THE PLEASURES
OF AN ABSENTEE LANDLORD
AND OTHER ESSAYS

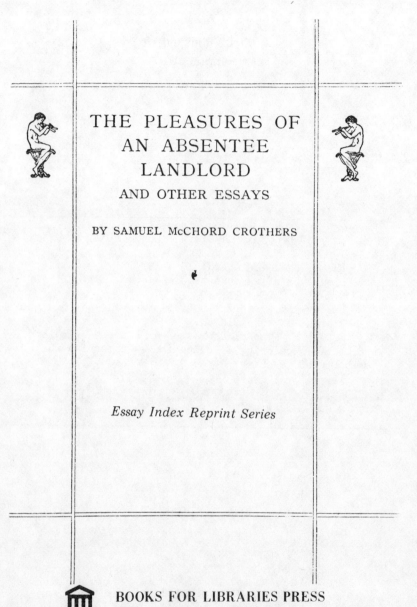

THE PLEASURES OF
AN ABSENTEE
LANDLORD
AND OTHER ESSAYS

BY SAMUEL McCHORD CROTHERS

Essay Index Reprint Series

BOOKS FOR LIBRARIES PRESS
FREEPORT, NEW YORK

First Published 1916
Reprinted 1972

Library of Congress Cataloging in Publication Data

Crothers, Samuel McChord, 1857-1927.
    Pleasures of an absentee landlord.

    (Essay index reprint series)
    Reprint of the 1916 ed.
    CONTENTS: The pleasures of an absentee landlord.--
Protective coloring in education.--Concerning the
liberty of teaching. [etc.]
    I. Title.
PS3505.R9P6 1972   814'.5'2   72-1326
ISBN 0-8369-2844-X

PRINTED IN THE UNITED STATES OF AMERICA

CONTENTS

THE PLEASURES OF AN ABSENTEE LANDLORD: With *Remarks* on the *Irresponsible* reading of HISTORY.

IN the troubled history of Ireland the villain was the Absentee Landlord. Nothing good was ever said of him. He was a parasite for whom no apology could be made. The sum of his iniquities was that he enjoyed property without assuming any of the responsibilities that belonged to it.

In England he might be an excellent member of society, conscious of the duties of a citizen and neighbor. But his occasional visits to his estates across St. George's Channel were not even for the purpose of collecting his rents — that he left to his agents. With some careless companions he would spend a rollicking fortnight or two among his tenantry, receive their "God bless you's," for nothing at all, and then return to the serious business of life.

All this was very reprehensible, and justifies the reproaches which have been visited upon absentee landlordism. The pleasures of the absentee landlord were wicked pleasures, because they were gained at the expense of others. But this is not to deny that they were real pleasures. Property plus responsibility is a serious matter. Irresponsible ownership is a rose without a thorn. If we can come by it honestly and without any detriment to others, we are to be congratulated.

The most innocent form in which this unmoral pleasure can be enjoyed is in the ownership of an abandoned farm. Of course one must satisfy his social conscience by making sure that the agricultural derelict was abandoned for good cause, and that the former owner bettered his condition by moving away. In the mountain regions of New England it is not difficult to find such places. At the gate of the hill farm the genuine farmer stands aside and says to the summer resident, "After you."

To one who possesses a bit of such land, the charm lies in the sense of irresponsibility. One can without compunction do what he will with his own, with the comfortable assurance that no one could do much better.

When as an Absentee Landlord I run up to my ragged, unkempt acres on a New Hampshire hilltop, I love to read the Book of Proverbs with their insistence on sleepless industry.

"I went by the field of the slothful . . . and lo! it was all grown over with thorns; and nettles had covered the face thereof and the stone wall thereof was broken down."

What a perfect description of my estate!

"Then I saw and considered it well. I looked upon it and received instruction . . ."

The sluggard saith, "Yet a little sleep and a little slumber, a little folding of the hands in sleep. So shall poverty come as one that travelleth."

I say, How true! If I had to make my living by farming, these words would stir me to agricultural effort. But as it is, they have a soothing sound. If my neighbor does n't like the wild blackberries, that is his misery, not mine. I prefer the picturesque, broken-down wall to his spick-and-span one.

If he asks why, I will not reason with him;

for does not the proverb say, " The sluggard is wiser in his own conceit than seven men that can render a reason " ?

That is the way I feel. I propose for several weeks in the year to be a sluggard with all the rights and privileges appertaining thereto.

" The sluggard will not plough by reason of the cold, therefore in harvest he shall have nothing."

My experience confirms this. But then I did not expect to have anything.

"By much slothfulness the building decayeth."

This also I observe, not without a certain measure of quiet satisfaction. The house is not what it used to be. How much less stiff and formal everything is under the mellowing influence of time. Nature corrects our tendency to deal too exclusively in straight lines. What an improvement has come with that slight sag in the roof. How much more lovable the shingles are than in their self-assertive youth. What an artist the weather is in the matter of staining. It is an Old Master retouching the work of the village painter. Nature is toning down the mistakes of man. A little sleep and a little slumber, and the house will cease to be a blot on the landscape.

I should not like to feel that way all the year, for I am a great believer in the industrial virtues when they keep their place. When I observe people who feel that way all the time, I feel like remonstrating with them. When I observe people who never feel that way, I do not remonstrate with them — it would do no good. But I like now and then to escape from their company.

The pleasure which one gets out of the ownership of an abandoned farm is of the same kind which one may get out of history. I am not speaking of history as it appears to the serious historian. He is engaged in a business which demands conscientious industry. The past is to him a field of research, and it must be cultivated intensively if he is to get valuable results. He is never free from the sense of responsibility.

But because the serious historian is virtuous and follows scientific methods, shall there be no cakes and ale for those who require only to refresh their minds by little excursions into the past? They do not desire to interfere with business nor to trespass on cultivated fields. They are in holiday mood, and desirous only of getting away from the humdrum life into a region where they may have a liberating sense of irresponsibility.

A recent congress of historians was congratulated on the progress which had been made "since history ceased to be a pleasant branch of literature and has become the work of eager and conscientious specialists." Now one may admire the work of these conscientious specialists and yet see no reason why history as a pleasant branch of literature should cease. In the present there is room both for work and for play. One may go to his office or he may go fishing without losing his right to live. Why may one not have the same liberty in regard to time past?

The scientific historian may ask, if recreation is what is wanted, why does not the vacationist content himself with the historical romances provided for just such idle persons? The answer is that it is not romance but reality with which he wishes to come into contact. Only he wants to enjoy his reality in his own care-free way.

Our real motive for going into the past, if we are allowed to confess it frankly, is to get away from our contemporaries. If our sole object were to acquire a stock of useful knowledge, we should be inclined to stay where we are and confine our attention to the facts of the present time, which we may learn by personal observation.

But to live all the time among our contemporaries is not good for us. They may be excellent people, but there are too many of them, and they are always standing around waiting to do something for us or have us do something for them. They are at once our collaborators and our critics. We can have no relations with our contemporaries that do not involve responsibilities. If we do one thing, we must do something else to match it. If we express a good thought, our contemporaries will demand a good act to correspond. If we express an interest in a worthy cause, they at once present us with a subscription paper. A good word is a promise to pay, and when it comes due we may not be prepared to meet our obligations.

After a while we are in danger of becoming

Malthusians. It seems as if the population of duties increased faster than the means of moral subsistence. It is all very well to say: "Look out and not in." But when we do so we must expect to hear the next admonition, "Lend a hand." When both hands are full, looking out ceases to be a pleasure.

It is in the attempt at self-protection that danger to our spontaneity comes. The man who finds it increasingly difficult to make both ends meet, morally speaking, begins to economize in his thinking and feeling. He does not wish to make the acquaintance of new thoughts that might involve new expenditures. He will not intrude himself on ideals that are above his station in life.

In the hand-to-mouth struggle for existence he cuts off all luxuries and develops a standardized intelligence. This makes him safe but uninteresting. That does not matter to him, so long as he is young, for then he is at least interesting to himself. But, after a time, even that solace fails him. His state is that indicated in the familiar reports of the stock market — "Narrow, Dull, and Firm."

It is when we are in danger of falling into this state that the call of the past comes to us. It is like the call of the woods and mountains. We can there see things going on without being responsible for the outcome. By getting away from our contemporaries we can be care-free spectators of the play of human forces. Not being able to do anything about it, we can have the satisfaction of seeing what it is really like.

With our contemporaries we cannot indulge in the luxury of seeing both sides. For we have to take one side and stick to it valiantly. We cannot get on sympathetic terms with bandits and bigots and other interesting characters, for we should be liable to encourage them in their wrongdoing. We must either approve or disapprove heartily, which is fatal to the process of understanding. But if we make the acquaintance of persons in another generation, we can enter into their point of view with impunity.

I remember how in the Excelsior Society we used to debate the question: "Was the execution of Mary Queen of Scots justifiable?" Sometimes we thought it was, and sometimes we thought it wasn't. We changed sides in the most shameful fashion. We had not the slightest compunction in telling anything we found out. There were no prudential considerations. We knew that the execution had taken place long ago, and no mistakes which we might make would prejudice the case.

And there was the question: "Was the career of Napoleon Bonaparte beneficial to Europe?" We reveled in the contradictory facts which we discovered. There was so much to be said on both sides. Nothing Napoleonic was alien to us of the Excelsior Society. We might debate on this subject for many moons, and the arguments would not lose their zest. But had we been living in France in the time of Napoleon, we should not have experienced these fine and stimulating pleasures. We should have been confined strictly to one side of the controversy. If we had attempted to argue that the career of Napoleon Bonaparte was not altogether beneficial to Europe, we should have speedily learned that the expression of this opinion was not beneficial to us. These prudential considerations would have severely limited the activities of our minds.

Have you never noticed the intellectual improvement that comes to a statesman who has survived his generation, and in his care-free old age writes reminiscences of a time that has now passed into history? When he was in office he never had a chance to express his personal opinions. He did not dare to say anything that might be misunderstood by his contemporaries, or have a bad effect on the next election. But now he is able to think and to speak freely. It is the blessed sense of irresponsibility that produces this result.

Some easy method of getting away from one's own time is desirable. I saw in a newspaper a suggestion from an inventive person in a Pennsylvania valley that we might utilize the rotation of the earth to reduce the cost of travel. His notion of the law of gravitation was more simple than that of most men of science, and he evidently imagined that it was something easily evaded. His plan was to rise in a balloon a few miles and stand still while the globe whirled round. All the traveler had to do was to adopt a policy of watchful waiting. When Samarcand or Jerusalem came into view beneath him, he

would descend and make himself at home. In
traveling through Space there are objections to
this plan on the score of practicability. But it
represents the way we may travel through Time.
All we have to do is to detach ourselves from
the present and drop into any century which
attracts our attention. We find interesting people who are doing interesting things. We may
listen to their talk and share their enthusiasms.

It is a great pleasure to have a little place in
the Past to which we may go with the care-free
mind of the Absentee Landlord. We have no
responsibility for its being as it is. We do not
feel in conscience bound to improve it.

Though the Absentee Landlord is not industrious or conscientious, there is one thing that
should commend him to the scientific historian.
He prefers original sources to the formal re-
constructions made at a later period. As his
pleasure consists in making a past period
seem present to him, he wishes to come into
direct contact with the people who were then
alive. He is not interested so much in the
sequence of events as in people and their
thoughts. He wants to know, not only what

they did, but how they felt when they were doing it. He does not much care for the historian, who is like the man with the megaphone in the "Seeing New York" motor-bus, who tells his passengers what they ought to see, while the bus moves so rapidly that they can't see it.

He does not care for the kind of history that does not take us away from our own time at all, but is simply a projection of contemporary ideas upon the past.

Here is a book published in the early nineteenth century which illustrates a certain way of imparting historical information. It was written with the intention of making history interesting to persons who did not want to venture into the Unfamiliar. It is a "History of the Patriarchs." The author evidently thought that if the patriarchs were conceived of as New England selectmen they could be made as interesting as if they were really New England selectmen. And I am not sure but that he succeeded. The book is divided into two parts: a conversation with Adam covering the space of nine hundred and thirty years, and an interview with Noah giving an account of the Deluge and other events with

which he was familiar. They are represented
as nice old gentlemen, strictly orthodox in
opinion. Adam speaks hopefully of Methu-
selah, who, he says, "must now be about fifty-
seven years old and is a discreet and well-
principled youth." He was much disturbed over
the Tubal-Cains, who had taken to radical views
and were becoming lax in their church attendance. There was nothing in the book to indicate
that either Adam or Noah had ever been out of
Connecticut.

The "History of Influenza" is a book produced on the same principle. The author, who,
it is needless to say, was a physician, instead of
giving a first-hand account of the influenzas he
had known, chose to treat his subject historically.
It is the necessity of keeping up the impression
of consecutiveness that wearies us. After one
has followed the influenza from the Greek and
Roman period, through the Dark Ages, the
Renaissance and the Protestant Reformation,
human history seems one prolonged sneeze. But
in all this historical excursion one feels that in
reality he has been made acquainted with nothing that he could not have found at home.

Many historical monographs are open to the same objection. The historian starts with a modern political or economic theory, then he searches the records of the past for instances to support it. The facts once discovered and verified, he fits them together with mechanical precision, and lo, a new history!

There is no question about the facts presented. They are chosen to illustrate his thesis. But I cannot help thinking of the innumerable little facts which he leaves out. They were very much alive once. My heart yearns for these non-elect infants.

The Absentee Landlord, having no modern axe to grind, can accept the facts that fit into no formal scheme. He is not responsible for their existence, and having resolved to do no manner of work he can indulge in idle curiosity. There being no possibility of improving the people he meets with, he can, without self-reproach, take time to see them as they are themselves.

Our pleasure in observing the fashions of our own day is marred by the fact that we may be expected to follow them. If we disapprove of them, it may be interpreted as being an admission that we are not as young as we once were.

If we go to an exhibition of pictures which purport to be the latest word in Art, we are not free in the expression of our opinion. The artist or his friends may be near at hand. When we are told that the artist is not portraying an actual scene, but only painting the state of his own mind, we hasten away. Perhaps that state of mind is catching. But in even the evil fashions of a generation that has completely passed away there is no danger. We may be rid of all ignoble fear of contagion. The passage of time has brought immunity. We may share the confidences of old-time sinners without any uneasy sense that we are compounding a felony.

Nor do variations of moral standards trouble us when we are relieved from the thought that they are likely to affect any one for whom we are responsible.

I find satisfaction in dropping into the year 1675 and taking up a little pamphlet, "The Discovery of Witches, by Mathew Hopkins, witch-finder, for the benefit of the whole kingdom." I can read Mathew Hopkins's plea for the restoration of his business without any irritation. I can really get his point of view. Mathew Hopkins was not a fanatic or a theorist. He was a businesslike person who had taken up the trade of witch-finding as another man might be a plumber. He was not an extremist. He utterly denied that the confession of a witch was of any validity if it was drawn from her by torture or violence. It was the practical side of witchcraft that interested him. When he took up the business of witch-finding, it was on a sound basis and offered a living for an industrious and frugal practitioner. But now the business is in a bad way. Whatever people may think, there is no money in it.

How pathetic is the statement of present-day conditions. Mr. Hopkins "demands but twenty shillings a town, and doth sometimes ride twenty miles for that, and hath no more for his charges thither and back again (and it may be stayes a weeke there) and finds there three or four witches, or it may be but one. Cheap enough! And this is the greate sum he takes to maintain his companie, with three horses!"

That touch of honest sarcasm makes me understand Mathew Hopkins. He is so sure that something is wrong, and so impervious to any considerations not connected with shillings and pence. That the business depression was connected with a great intellectual revolution did not occur to him. How pale all rationalistic arguments must have seemed to a man with three horses eating their heads off in the stables!

If Mathew Hopkins were living to-day, I should not permit myself to sympathize with him in his business perplexities, even to the extent of trying to understand how a man in his position would feel. But I have not the slightest fear that the business of witch-finding will be revived on any commercial scale. So from the security of the twentieth century I am able to look upon Mathew Hopkins as a human being. From that period of view I am able to see the resemblance between him and many other human beings of my acquaintance. A great many of them are better than their business.

A formal history of witchcraft does not give me the same intimate sense of it as does Matthew Hopkins's dry business like statement. He was actually making his living by it. My imagination is not strong enough to make a witch riding at midnight seem real. But the witch-finder is flesh and blood.

The historians, in attempting to give us an account of the movements of masses, fail to awaken human interest. The historian in the Book of Mormon, in his narrative of the tribal wars, complains of the difficulty of his task: —

"Now there were many records kept of the proceedings of this people, by many of this people, which are particular and very large concerning them. But behold a hundredth part of the proceedings of this people, yea the account of the Lamanites and of the Nephites and their wars and contentions and dissensions, and their preaching and their prophecies, and their building of ships and building of temples and synagogues, and their sanctuaries and their righteousness, and their wickedness and their robbings and plunderings and all manner of abominations cannot be contained in this work. But behold there are many books, and many records of every kind, and they have been chiefly kept by the Nephites."

There you have the real difficulty in writing a history of the Lamanites. There is plenty of material, indeed, too much of it. The generalities like wars and contentions and building of temples and robbings and plunderings become monotonous unless you have some inkling as to what sort of people did these things. You cannot trust the Nephites to give the Lamanitish point of view. For myself I should rather have a chance to meet a single Lamanite and hear his own account of himself than to be told of the manifold "proceedings" of his tribe. For one thing, it would quiet the doubt as to whether there ever was a Lamanite.

It is the little things, and not the big things, which make me feel at home. The historical personage must be something more than the symbol of a movement before we have a feeling that he belongs to us.

St. Basil the Great was to me but one of the Greek Fathers till I came across a familiar letter which he wrote to his friend Antipater, the Governor of Cappadocia. Since then he has been a very real person. Basil is writing, not about heresies but about pickled cabbage, which his friend Antipater had recommended for its health-giving qualities. He has heretofore been prejudiced against it as a vulgar vegetable, but now that it has worked such wonders with his friend he will esteem it equal to the ambrosia of the gods — whatever that may be. This is an excellent introduction to St. Basil. Starting the conversation with pickled cabbage, one can easily lead up to more serious subjects.

If it happens that we can make any little discovery of our own and find it confirmed by somebody in a previous generation, it puts us at our ease and forms a natural means of approach. It is always wise to provide for such introductions to strangers. Thus, though I am not a smoker, I like to carry matches in my pocket. One is always liable to be accosted on the street by some one in need of a light. To be able to give a match is a great luxury. It forms the basis for a momentary friendship.

One is often able to have that same feeling toward some one who would otherwise be a mere historical personage. My acquaintance with Lord Chesterfield came about in that way. Several years ago I wrote an essay for the "Atlantic Monthly" on "The Hundred Worst Books." For a place on the list I selected a book in my library entitled "Poems on Several Occasions," published in 1749, by one Jones, a poet altogether unknown to me till I perused his verse. The pages were so fresh that I cherished the belief that I was the only reader in a century and a half. I had the pride of possession in Jones.

It was some time after that I came across, in Walpole's letters, an allusion to my esteemed poet. It seems that Colley Cibber, when he thought he was dying, wrote to the Prime Minister, "recommending the bearer, Mr. Henry Jones, for the vacant laurel. Lord Chesterfield will tell you more of him."

I was never more astonished in my life than when I visualized the situation, and saw my friend Jones, the bearer of a demand for the reversion to the laureateship.

It seemed that Walpole was equally surprised, and when he next met Lord Chesterfield the eager question was, Who was Jones, and why should he be recommended for the position of poet laureate? Lord Chesterfield answered, "A better poet would not take the post and a worse ought not to have it." It appears that Jones was an Irish bricklayer and had made it his custom to work a certain number of hours according to an undeviating rule. He would lay a layer of brick and then compose a line of poetry, and so on till his day's task was over. This accounts for the marvelous evenness of his verse.

This was but a small discovery, but it gave a real pleasure, for should I meet my Lord Chesterfield, he and I would at once have a common interest. We both had discovered Jones, and quite independently.

Let no one think that these irresponsible sojournings in familiar parts of past time are recommended as substitutes for the painstaking work of conscientious historians. They are not. But they have a value of their own. The modest intention is to recover some point in the past and live in it as in the present, to leave our contemporaries and become the contemporaries of persons of another generation.

In order to do this we must share their limitations. That which is a peculiarity of the present is the extent of its environing ignorance. Something we may know of the past, but the future is hidden in the mists. In the story of the Creation "the evening and the morning were the first day." So it has been with each creative day. Each has its evening and its morning which wall it in, and keep it distinct from every other period of time. To live in any period we must preserve the sense of our evening and morning. We must rid our minds of that most confusing knowledge, the knowledge which comes after the event. The present would not be to us the present if we knew how everything was going to come out. We could not live and work in the face of absolute foreknowledge.

If we would become acquainted with Columbus, let us not begin with the announcement, "Christopher Columbus discovered America." That is twitting on facts. It suggests Plymouth Rock and the Battle of Bunker Hill and the Monroe Doctrine and all the things American the hardy Genoese seaman knew nothing about. He was not intending to discover America. His spirit was that of the Middle Ages. He was thinking of the Holy Sepulcher and of Cipango and the Great Khan. He dreamed a dream that did not come true, though other things happened which in the retrospect seem more important to us.

When after civil commotions a government seeks to restore order, it passes an act of oblivion. The transgressions of the past are wisely treated as non-existent, and the rebels of yesterday may go about without fear. To restore order into any period of history, we must pass an act of oblivion, not in regard to the past, but in regard to all that to the men of that time lay in the future.

Only then do all sorts of interesting facts come out of hiding. We begin to do justice to the endeavors of men whom we may have thought of as foes to progress. In their day, and according to their lights, they were progressives.

They were doing something necessary and they did it enthusiastically. It was not their fault that in the next generation the progress of civilization was in a different direction. That was the work of

> Reckoning Time, whose millioned accidents
> Creep in twixt vows to change decrees of kings,
> Tan sacred virtue, blunt the sharp'st intents
> And divert strong minds to course of altering things.

Amid the course of altering things it is pleasant and profitable to be able to watch the human reactions, not only of strong minds, but of average minds. And when we come back to our own times, we may be able to watch current events with more equanimity.

After all, the test of a vacation is the renewed zest with which we take up our work on our return. The person who lives among his contemporaries all the time has no idea how interesting they are. They appear even romantic after a short trip abroad.

Of course we must take up our responsibilities again. Our serious business with our contemporaries is to improve their morals and their manners. But before we begin again to improve them, we may enjoy the moment when we have enough freshness of vision to see them as they are.

PROTECTIVE COLORING IN EDUCATION

NATURALISTS have long noted the way in which various animals merge themselves into the landscape of which they form a part. It takes sharp eyes to distinguish the living thing from its environment. There are butterflies that look like the leaves on which they alight, caterpillars that resemble the bark of the tree they infest. The polar bear is a part of the snow-fields. Even the stripes of the zebra, which make him conspicuous in the circus, are said to be inconspicuous when seen against the arid landscape of South Africa.

All these concealments are useful in the struggle for existence. They form part of the grand strategy of Nature. The creature unable to stand in the open against its enemies seeks to escape their prying eyes. It tries to look like something else.

These natural hypocrisies throw light on human conduct. When we call a man a hypocrite, we usually assume that he is trying to imitate a higher order of being than that to which he has actually attained. In this we perhaps do too much credit to his spiritual ambition.

The hypocrisies in Nature are not of this kind. The creature does not imitate its betters but its inferiors. The vegetable imitates the mineral; the animal imitates the vegetable. It does not parade its peculiar talents, but modestly slips back in the scale of being. It likes to hide in the already existing.

The naturalists distinguish between protective coloring of animals — that which they call cryptic coloring — and mimicry. The cryptic coloring aims purely at concealment. In mimicry the hunted creature finds safety in its resemblance to some other creature which is either feared or disliked or despised. Thus, a worm which is really good to eat escapes the predatory bird by looking like a worm that is not good to eat. It willingly sacrifices its reputation for gastronomic excellence in order to prolong its existence.

Harmless, good-natured reptiles wriggle along

in peace because they superficially resemble venomous snakes with whom interiorly they have nothing in common. Any one who has made the acquaintance of a garden toad knows that he is not nearly so ugly as he looks. After thousands of years of precarious living, these wise amphibians have learned to divest themselves of the fatal gift of beauty. Doubtless the less unprepossessing attracted the attention of envious rivals and were slain, while those whom none could envy survived.

One who takes a sympathetic view of the evolutionary process will make allowance for the many worthy creatures who conceal their virtues from prudential reasons. They are like a richly freighted merchantman trying to avoid capture. It receives a coat of paint to match the fog, extinguishes its lights, and makes a run to avoid the enemies' cruisers.

An appreciation of the ways of the hunted would save the ambitious educator from many disappointments. He is engaged in the imparting of knowledge, the holding-up of ideals, the development of the higher faculties. Being human, he longs to see the results of his labors.

What becomes of the embryo scholars and philosophers and social reformers when they begin to shift for themselves?

Ah, there comes the bitter disappointment. These objects of tremulous care, the moment they are released from tutelage, seem to lose their painfully acquired superiority. Instead of proudly carrying their educational advantages as an oriflamme of progress, they carefully conceal them, and take the color of their present world.

The enthusiastic kindergartner one day visits the primary school to see how her little graduates are following the ideals she has imparted with such loving care. Little George Augustus was the paragon of the kindergarten. With wide-open eyes and eager ears he received the sweet parables of Nature, and with nimble fingers practiced what he had been taught. None in the kindergarten so docile as he. To him education would be no task. With his heart so early attuned to its harmonies he would joyfully play upon it, as on an instrument of ten strings.

But alas. In the public school little George Augustus does not stand out as one of the elect infants. The multiplication table has for him no spiritual meaning, and against its literal meaning he hardens his heart. His realistic mind does not in the least mistake work for play. He perceives instantly and resentfully where one begins and the other leaves off. His attitude is that of his fellow conspirators. He will learn his lesson if he has to, but he will not encourage teacher by performing any work of supererogation.

Has the kindergarten failed? Not ultimately. The effects will doubtless reappear; but they are now in hiding. George Augustus is wise in his generation. Through several weeks of hard experience in his new environment he has learned to appear as one of the unkindergartened. His newly acquired manners are the protective coloring which enables him to go about unmolested.

A distinguished physiologist has shown by a number of experiments that terror and hate produce the same physiological reactions. In the one case the instinct is to get away from the foe; in the other it is to get at him. In either case there is a demand made on the adrenal glands, which, as a war measure, pour adrenaline into the blood. In the case of little George Augustus, the sudden increase of adrenaline which makes him appear so truculent is produced, not by hate of sound learning, but by a well-founded fear. He is panic-stricken over the possibility of being called "Teacher's Pet."

I have in mind a boy who was early taught to love to go to Sunday school and hear the Sabbath bell. At the age of ten he suddenly informed his parents, with the air of a hardened offender, that he intended to cut Sunday school regularly once a month. On inquiry it appeared that the Superintendent had arranged an honor list on which were to be inscribed the names of those whose attendance for a month had been faultless.

"Dickey says he got caught that way once." There was something not to be endured in the thought of standing before his companions as a horrible example of the degrading virtue of punctuality.

The youth who passes from an excellent preparatory school into the university has the same experience. He has an uneasy feeling that he has been overeducated. The whole of the freshman year is sometimes spent in the successful attempt to conceal the too careful training he has received. Only when he is convinced by the College Office that his attainments do not make him conspicuous, does he feel that he may safely continue his education.

The educator who would keep a cheerful courage up must be something of a detective. He must be able to penetrate the disguises which his pupils put on to conceal from him the result of his labors among them. He must remember that these youthful pilgrims are traveling through an unfriendly world. To some of them, the intellectual life is an uncanny thing of which they have heard in the classroom, but of which they are suspicious. It appears to them as the field of psychical research does to the partially convinced. When the conditions are right, the phenomena appear. But when they go on the street and talk with the uninitiated, they mention these matters with a tone of indifference. They do not like to appear too credulous.

Moreover, these young people are conscious that their stay in the seats of learning is but temporary. They are aware that the subjects in which the university seeks to interest them are not mentioned in the good society which they aspire to enter. Were they to acquire any unusual ideas, they fear that on their return to their native Philistia they might be interned as alien enemies.

Education depends, not only on the consent of those who are being educated, but on the consent of those who are paying the bills. The proud father is willing to pay roundly for an education which will make his son like himself. It is hard to make him appreciate an education which aims to produce a salutary unlikeness.

The only institutions which can openly avow their real ambitions for betterment are those which are endowed and supported for the benefit of confessedly backward races. Carlisle Institute for the Indians does not profess to make its students like their fathers. It boldly admits to the paternal relatives that it sees room for improvement. The student is not to go back to take up the accustomed life in the wigwam. He is to tear down the wigwam and make a civilized home.

But this would not be so easy if the school had to depend for its support on the Indian tribes from which the pupils come. Some self-made savage of the old school would declare that he would have no flummery fit only for molly-coddles. In the interest of efficiency he would endow a chair of practical scalping.

The Indian school is like a system of waterworks fed from a remote and elevated reservoir. All one has to do is to turn the water on and let it flow through the pipes. But the institution of higher education for the more favored classes has no such advantage. It is like the hydraulic ram placed in the bed of the running stream. Most of the water that runs through it escapes downhill, but in doing so sends a very slender stream far above its natural level.

It is the function of the institution of higher learning to educate the public that supports it up to the point of appreciating its real purpose. But while it is being educated up to this point, will the public support it? That is a matter that causes anxious thought.

Athens supported a numerous body of sophists who taught what the Athenians wanted to know. Socrates had a different educational ideal. He endeavored to teach the Athenians that they didn't know a good many things they thought they knew. This method was not so readily appreciated.

Have you ever heard a successful business man who is also a real philanthropist address his fellow business men in regard to his pet projects? Does he confess himself as of the tribe of Abou Ben Adhem? Not at all. He gloats over the fact that, whatever else he may be, he is not a philanthropist. He has but one thought in his hard head, and that is, "Business is business." He refers admiringly to "brass tacks," and declares that whatsoever is not brass tacks is vanity. He is a confirmed money-getter, and despises anything that doesn't pay.

After having thus allayed suspicion, he unfolds his plans. He has shrewdly outwitted his employees and doubled their salaries, by which means he expects to treble their efficiency. He intends to invest this unearned increment in various schemes for public health and recreation. By investments of this kind he will make the community so prosperous and optimistic that they just can't help buying his goods. Yes, sir, it pays in dollars and cents to enlarge one's business in this way. It pays.

All this is protective coloring. In his heart the public-spirited hypocrite knows that he would do these things whether they paid or not.

The phenomena of protective coloring are seen, not only in the way in which the educational world takes on the color of the business or social world that surrounds it; they are seen in the way in which any new interest hides behind some interest or discipline that has already been established. The new idea seldom appears in its true colors. It adopts some prudential disguise.

One thing which prevents the full realization of the ideal of liberal culture is the difficulty of keeping one branch of study from interfering with another. Nowhere is it more true that one good custom will corrupt the world. With all the bewildering variety of courses the student is often taught only one way of using his mind. Usually there is one method or discipline that exercises an autocratic power. Everything must take color from that.

There was a time when Theology was the recognized Queen of the Sciences. Education was in the hands of the clergy. Woe unto the teacher of youth who did not theologize — or seem to theologize.

The physical sciences had to walk warily and conceal their identity from the prying eyes of the ecclesiastical police. In the gardens of learning, brute facts were not admitted unless held in leash by some sound doctrine. Science pure and simple did not come out in the open and display its miscellaneous assortment of undogmatic actualities. A man could hardly be a professor of such things. But by professing to be something else, he might dispense useful knowledge of selected physical facts.

Paley's "Natural Theology" contained a considerable amount of information about anatomy and physiology. Its initial reference to the watch might furnish a text for one interested in mechanics. Priestley, as a preacher and theologian, — though heterodox, — made valuable discoveries in chemistry. It was to his credit that he discovered oxygen, an element not easily discoverable in meeting-houses. But the contributions to science were incidental. The approach was furtive. By indirections they found direction out. We are reminded of the text in the Book of Judges: "In the days of Shamgar the son of Anoth, the highways were deserted and the people walked in byways." The timid folk who walked in these scientific byways made no display of intellectual wealth. All they hoped for was to escape notice.

They were fortunate if they could make their favorite studies look like something else. In the days of Hugh Miller, Geology disguised itself as a useful commentary on the first chapters of Genesis. It was a branch of Hermeneutics — the science of the interpretation of texts. If the testimony of the rocks confirmed the texts —so much the better for the rocks.

Tennyson preserves the memory of the situation : —

Half awake I heard
The parson taking wide and wider sweeps,
Now harping on the Church Commission,
Now hawking at Geology and Schism.

The scientific man had not only to suffer many things from dogmatic theologians, but he was also in bondage to literary taskmasters.

When the educational world was ruled by those whose interests were primarily literary and classical, he had a hard time of it. For literary values and scientific values do not coincide. Literature is concerned with certain proprieties and congruities and dramatic unities. A story need not be literally true, but it must be well told. An idea, to be received in good society, must be clothed and in its right mind.

In the Dame School of Literature, facts are not received simply as facts. They must mind their manners. They must wipe their feet on the mat, and learn how to come into the room. If they do not come in properly, the Dame sends them out to try it again.

There is something pathetic in the way in which the scientifically minded tried to conform to these requirements of polite learning. In the darkest recesses of old bookstores you will find shelves full of semi-scientific, semi-sentimental volumes published in the early nineteenth century. They are intended to insinuate knowledge of the physical world under all sorts of literary disguises. The theory is that the reader will not mind fact if it is presented as if it were not a fact.

HERE is a novel, Alonzo and Melissa, by a long-forgotten Connecticut writer, who in the preface ventures a timid hope that the story may serve to increase our knowledge of nature, while at the same time pointing a useful moral to the young.

Alonzo and Melissa are making love as they sit on the shores of Long Island Sound. As Alonzo is proposing to Melissa, they are aware that they should pay attention to natural phenomena. So they endeavor to cultivate observation and improve their minds in this fashion.

Melissa. "See that ship. How she ploughs through the white foam, while the breeze flutters the sails, varying the beams of the sun."

Alonzo. "Yes, it is almost down."

Melissa. "What is almost down?"

Alonzo. "The sun. Was not you speaking of the sun, madam?"

Melissa. "Your mind is absent, Alonzo. I was speaking of yonder ship."

Alonzo. "I beg pardon, madam; oh, yes, the ship. See how it bounds with rapid motion over the waves."

In some such absent-minded fashion did the

Melissas and Alonzos study what was called natural philosophy. It allowed plenty of time in which to think of something else.

It is interesting to remember that Charles Darwin was the grandson of Dr. Erasmus Darwin, who was also a man of scientific attainments. But when, in 1789, Dr. Darwin sought to express his ideas on botany, he did it in such a way as not to alarm the Melissas and Alonzos. He sought to introduce botany into the most select circles of the world of polite learning in an elaborate poem called "The Loves of the Plants." He sought to insinuate the Linnæan system through the romantic adventures of gnomes and sylphs and nereids and other well-known classical characters. More detailed botanical information was given in the notes.

Miss Anna Seward, known as the "Swan of Lichfield," and a very great literary lady of her day, says of Dr. Darwin's poem: "The genuine charm of his muse must endure as long as the English language shall exist. Should that perish, translation would preserve the Botanic Garden as one of its gems. . . . Can anything be finer than the description of the signs of the zodiac?

Or that passage describing the calcining of the phlogistic ores which is termed the marriage of Ether with the Mine? The passage is most poetic though purely chemical."

Miss Seward followed with unabated admiration the wooing of the various flowers, under which pleasant disguise the most abstruse botanical information was conveyed. "The pictures of the various flowers arise in the page in botanic discrimination, and all the hues of poetry." In the description of the love-making of the flax, Miss Seward says: "We are presented with the exactest description, not only of the growth of flax, but the weaving of linen. Sir Richard Arkwright's apparatus at Matlock is described." Other machinery is described. "We have in sweet versification the whole process of this admirable invention. It is an encouragement to science that this bard throws over them all the splendid robe of descriptive poetry." In treating the transformation of the vine into a bacchanalian female, Dr. Darwin introduces the subject of temperance. Says Miss Seward, "The many disorders of the liver caused by ebriety are nobly allegorized."

Not only the more romantic floweis, but vegetable growths of lowlier order are allegorized nobly. Miss Seward is enraptured by a delightful passage about truffles. "The Truffle, a well-known fungus, now meets our attention as a fine lady. She is married to a gnome in a grand subterranean palace, soothed by the music of æolian strings, which make love to the tender echoes in the circumjacent caves, while cupids hover around and shake celestial day from their bright lamps."

In such disguises did the grandfather of Charles Darwin introduce natural science to the polite world of his generation.

All this belongs to the past. The physical sciences have won their place in the sun. Having won their independence, they now aspire to imperial rule. The scientific method is everywhere being rigidly enforced.

Our sympathies with the under-dog lead us to inquire into the state of the older forms of culture which are now passing under a foreign yoke.

Literature, philosophy, ethics, and the fine

arts existed in prescientific days, and flourished mightily. Each had a discipline and method of its own. Each gathered about itself a band of votaries who loved it for its own sake, and were satisfied with its own rewards.

Time was when the philosopher walked in a grove with a group of eager youths who shared his curiosity about the universe. He liked to talk with them about the whence and the whither and the why of everything. They were frankly speculative. They asked questions which they were well aware admitted of no definite and final answer. They disputed with one another for the sheer joy of intellectual conflict. The disputations sharpened their wits, but they "got no results." In fact they were not seeking any results that an efficiency expert could recognize. The free use of their minds was joy enough.

Now, it is evident that a modern university is too serious a place for much of this sort of thing. Life is too short, and business is business, and time is money. Youth must be up and doing, and not lose its opportunities by meditating overmuch on the ultimate reason of things.

Still, it seems to me that in the most efficient

university there ought to be room for at least one philosopher, and he should not be compelled to teach philosophy by the "scientific method." He should be allowed to practice the philosophic method, which is really an excellent one for its own purpose.

There is something a little pathetic in seeing a real philosopher trying to teach a company of busy undergraduates, who have never learned to meditate. "May we not say of the philosopher," asks Plato, "that he is a lover, not of a part of wisdom, but of the whole?"

The philosopher, finding himself in an intellectual community where the interests are highly specialized, becomes a little uneasy and self-conscious. In order to be in the fashion he must appear to be a specialist also. And so he frequently disguises his real aim by a critical apparatus which imposes on the undiscerning. It is all the more refreshing when we come across a philosopher who is interested in the incomprehensible universe, and who does n't care who knows it.

The plight of the teacher of literature is somewhat different. He is afraid of the undue popularity of his courses among the less industrious undergraduates. He bears about with him a secret which is a source of personal joy, but at the same time full of danger to the uninitiated. It must be carefully guarded. This guilty secret is that the reading of good books, especially if they are written in one's native language, is not hard work, but is in reality a pleasant pastime. The masterpieces of literature are not difficult reading to any one who approaches them in the right spirit. They are often thrilling, they are sometimes amusing, and they are usually written in such a style that their meaning is easily grasped. First-rate books are written in a more understandable style than third-rate books. All this the teacher of literature well knows, and his secret desire is to lead appreciative youth in the paths of pleasantness which he has discovered.

But alas, if the secret were known, his classrooms would be invaded by a host of young Philistines in search of easy courses. "Tell it not in Gath, publish it not in the streets of Askelon!"

The pleasant paths must be obstructed by barbed-wire entanglements borrowed from the scientific machine shops. Instead of an invitation to read together the few books which are a joy forever, the "required reading" leads over many a long and rocky road chosen because it furnishes a good endurance test. It is hoped that the idle fellows will fall by the wayside, and the grapes of Canaan may be reserved for those who have crossed the forbidding desert.

Sometimes the teacher of literature wonders whether it is worth while to keep up the stern pretense. Why not let the cat out of the bag? Reading is a recreation rather than an enforced discipline. Why should not leisure be left for such recreation even in the strenuous days of youth? The habit will be a great solace in later life.

We are beginning to see that the ideal of a liberal education is too large to be put into four years of a college course. It is the growth of a lifetime spent in contact with the actual world. But it is not too much to ask that in a university the student should be brought into contact with different types of the intellectual life, and that each type should be kept distinct. He should learn that the human mind is a marvelous instrument and that it may be used in more than one way.

Variety in courses of study is less important than variety and individuality of mental action. How does a man of science use his mind? How does an artist feel? What makes a man a jurist, a man of business, a politician, a teacher? How does ethical passion manifest itself? What is the historical sense?

These are not questions to be answered on examination papers. But it is a reasonable hope that a young man in the formative period of his life may learn the answers through personal contacts.

CONCERNING THE LIBERTY OF TEACHING: Epaphroditus to his much-valued *Philosopher* and *Slave* Epictetus

THE gods, Epictetus, distribute their gifts as they will. To me they have given, through the favor of the divine Nero, freedom and wealth. On thee they have bestowed an acute understanding and a fervent love of wisdom. These are the more excellent gifts, for which thou art duly thankful. Had I been endowed with a virtuous disposition, I should have practiced those virtues which I have been pleased to hear thee describe. But it was not so decreed. I must be content with what a Christian slave, quoting from the scriptures of his sect, calls " filthy lucre."

But thou hast taught me that everything should be taken by its right handle. Grasping filthy lucre, with no unwilling hands, I may make it serve my purpose. If I cannot be a

philosopher — a state far above my poor deserts
— I can at least own one.

Other rich men invest their money in gladia-
tors, or charioteers, or dancing women, or in beautiful youths who attract the admiration of the un-
thinking. But I have soberer tastes. It is my
ambition to be the owner of a veritable philosopher, one who devotes himself continually to
the highest themes. When thou wert a mere boy,
I recognized thy worth. Here is one who has in
him the making of a sage. Give him but good
masters and leisure to grow wise, and I will
match him against any thinker in Rome. For
this end, I sent thee to the school of Musonius
Rufus, that thou mightest learn the lore of the
ancients. In my household I have given thee
every opportunity to practice frugality and all
the austere virtues of the Stoics, for I would train
thee to be a winner in the immortal race. Thou
art yet young, Epictetus, but thou art full of
promise.

Two thousand years from now, when the
Empire of the Cæsars has extended beyond the
western seas, who will remember the heroes of
the arena, or the rich men who supported them?

But in that far-off day men will speak of Epaphroditus. Was he not the lawful owner of the
great Epictetus?

Do not chide me for linking my name with
thine. I know that the desire for fame is something unbefitting a philosopher. But I am not a
philosopher. I am not thyself. I am only thy
proprietor. Do not blame me for this vanity.
It is in accordance with my nature. Thou knowest, as indeed all Rome knows, my vices. Do
not be too severe with this my imperfect virtue.

For it is a virtue, Epictetus, this admiration
for thy virtue. Thou knowest how highly I
value thee. I would not sell thee for the price
of a chariot and horses. And it is thy virtues
that make thee of such value to me. Often at
Nero's banquets I contrast thy temperance with
my luxury. Thou art able to sleep on a hard
bed, to wear coarse clothing, to eat sparingly
and to be content. How much better that is
than my satiety! How altogether admirable is
thy way of life! I should not think of attempting to imitate it. It is inimitable.

But I am grieved, Epictetus, to receive from
thee a letter in which for the first time I discern

a flaw in thy philosophy. Forgive me if I, who
am thy inferior in such high matters, call attention to it. For the first time thou hast shown dis-
contentment with thy lot. Thou sayest that the
question has arisen in thy mind whether a teacher
of philosophy should be a slave. What will
future generations say to a civilization in which
the man who knows submits to be the property
of the man who furnishes the means to support
his bodily existence? And will not people
distrust the teachings of a man who obeys another's will? What would Socrates say to such
a relation?

Ah, Epictetus! Are not such questions answered by thy philosophy? There are things indifferent. What does it matter what the vulgar
think of thee? Their thoughts cannot harm
thee. And what of Posterity? Posterity will
have troubles of its own, and doubtless will have
invented new forms of servitude, which may
make our system of slavery appear to err on the
side of too much freedom. As for Socrates, he
doubtless would have his bitter jibe. But he
lived in a tumultuous little city where liberty was
carried to excess, and not in a great ordered

Empire where Cæsar gives to every man his due. And Socrates would have lived longer if he had had a master who could have protected him from the results of his own vagaries. In his quiet old age, after he had seen the folly of asking so many questions, he might have written down the answers which were desirable. Had Socrates been the slave of Alcibiades, he might have lived to be his own Plato.

Slavery is an external condition. It is something which is not within thy power to change. Should it not be therefore accepted with equanimity? I myself am only a freedman, but I am now thy master, for I have been able, through the wealth that I have acquired, to buy thee. Should these outward things be allowed to fret thy soul?

Slavery is doubtless degrading to one who is not a philosopher. But to a philosopher it offers many opportunities for admirable self-renunciation. When one door is shut, another opens. I shut the door of the outer liberty against thee. Thou openest the door of the inner liberty, so that thou mightest enter a realm into which I am not worthy to follow thee. This certainly is to thy advantage. Does not freedom, for every one, have its limits? The soul is in a beautiful garden walled about by necessity. If it were not for the wall, the soul would wonder abroad and engage in futile conflicts with reality. If we were altogether free, we should act and not think. But Necessity compels us to think in order to explain why we do not achieve. It is a salutary experience. We attempt to do a good deed. Nature prevents. Then we think a good thought and find our satisfaction in that. Is not that the birth of Philosophy?

In regard to the business of life, let Epaphroditus stand to thee in the place of brute Nature. He shall be the lower limit to thy activity. Thy problem is to be as free as it is possible to be while yet his slave. He shall prevent thy powers from being wasted on matters unworthy of thee. In all that concerns thy higher life, thou shalt be free. When thy will conflicts with the will of Epaphroditus, thou mayest escape by a sudden flight into the upper air. He will watch thy furthest flight into pure virtue with approval. The further the better. Do not interfere with him and he will not interfere with thee.

Thou askest, "Why should Epaphroditus wish to own Epictetus when he makes so little use of his teachings in the conduct of his own life?"

Ah, Epictetus, thou little knowest what it is to be rich. To be very rich is to possess more than one can use. It is in the possession and not in the use that the possibility of any satisfaction comes. The man who has one horse rides it and finds enjoyment in the exercise. But the man who has a thousand horses cannot ride them all; perhaps he does not even see them. Such joys he leaves to those whom he employs for the purpose.

I have heard thee say that there are things that money cannot buy. I know that this is true. We poor wretches, who have nothing but the things which money can buy, must make the most of our poor possessions. While we cannot expect the finer joys, we accept the gratification that belongs to our situation.

To practice disinterested virtue is a privilege which is thine. I cannot enter into it. But do I not clothe thee, feed thee, and direct thy actions? In this sense of proprietorship I find a satisfaction which is a compensation for my own lack of participation in the moral life. To have in my own household a model of perfect virtue is a comfort to me, which I cannot explain. I am not inclined to conform to the model. May one not do what he will with his own, even to letting it alone?

Is not the matter reduced to this: the relation between the Wise and the Prosperous? Plato conceived a Republic in which the philosophers ruled. The truth-lover was allowed to play the tyrant. There could be no glad worship of Prosperity in such a community. Is it not better to allow each class to follow its own nature? Let the wise be wise and let the prosperous be prosperous.

Wherein does my prosperity interfere with thy wisdom? Thou art able to draw many lessons from my conduct. I am thy helot in whom thou canst find an excellent example of the evils of intemperance.

Let the wise practice reciprocity with the prosperous. It is a mistake to say that we ever prefer falsehood to truth or delight to surround ourselves with insincere flatterers. We prefer truth if we can only find the kind that serves our ends. Here is the opportunity for the wise. Let them cultivate many kinds of truth, so as to have something pleasing for every occasion. They should be prepared to present the truths that are called for. When Cæsar desires wine, the cup-bearer, with sure instinct, offers the wine that most accords with Cæsar's taste. It is not wine for its own sake, but wine for the sake of the imperial palate, that is demanded.

I have spoken of the man with a thousand horses. Since I have owned thee, Epictetus, I have sometimes dreamed of a School of a Thousand Sages. Were I rich enough, I would bring together the truly wise from the ends of the earth, so that they should advance human knowledge and present it in its endless variety. I would build great houses for my learned men and give them ample leisure to pursue their various studies. Hither should the youth of the Empire resort for instruction.

My scholars should be able to teach all that is known among men. In the great school there should be a thousand eager minds, and a single will. Not that I should use my will often.

Only it should be a power in reserve. I should know it was there, and my learned men should know it was there, and wisely avoid a conflict.

Of all the arts, Epictetus, Education seems to me the greatest, and the one that should be in the hands of the ruling class. The teacher is a sculptor whose statue is not passive under his hand. He is Pygmalion, whose masterpiece is alive. What power greater than to prepare a thought, and then skillfully prepare minds who will think that thought? The first thinker can thus multiply his thought indefinitely. He chooses his theme and his people with disciplined mentality follow him through all the mazes of prearranged harmony. There can be no discord between theory and practice when the theory has been made to fit the practice. When wise men are chosen and trained to teach that which is expedient, we have a human cosmos, a beautiful order. What one man thinks is negligible, but a million minds thinking rhythmically are irresistible.

If I were Cæsar — which it is blasphemy for me to imagine — I should build over against my Golden House a Temple of Learning, a

School of the Thousand Sages. He who builds his empire on Fear rules only over cowards. Some day, through his fostering care, his subjects grow strong and self-reliant and with one voice cry, Who is afraid? And when men cease to be afraid, the Empire falls.

But there is a power which coerces the strong. It is the power of Thought. Men will go through fire and water for an opinion. The ruler who would reign completely must gain control of men's opinions, and form them to his own will.

I fear Cæsar takes too little account of this. Only yesterday in the Arena I saw a fanatic torn to pieces because he held the opinion that Cæsar is not divine. A word or a gesture would have saved him, but the wretch chose to die in agony.

When the spectacle was over, Cæsar turned to me and said, "Poor fool, he might be alive and merry at this moment had he but understood that I care not a fig for what he thinks, but only for what he says."

I said, as was my duty, that the godlike Cæsar spoke with sublime wisdom. But within myself

I doubted. These wretches are unafraid. What if their opinion should spread throughout the Empire, till all men should think of Cæsar's power as a baseless superstition? Would Cæsar be supremely powerful if men did not think him so?

No, the Empire must be supported by intelligence. It must appeal to reason. I would have a Prætorian Guard of the learned to support my claims to the homage of mankind. These men should be trained to think together. Their thoughts should form a solid phalanx. When they move, it should be in unison and to a clearly defined object. My Empire should be to them the Cosmos, and my will the law of Nature. Beyond it should be only the realm of Chaos and Night, into which they would not think of intruding.

Then I should do what I willed, and none should ask why, because my sages would have anticipated the inquiry. Men would be taught the correct answers, before it occurred to them to ask the difficult question. They would have shown that it was not willfulness but necessity that caused the action: Cæsar being what he is, it is necessary that Cæsar's action should have been what it has been. When my sages had demonstrated that this is so, the people would be satisfied. For man is a rational animal and loves to have a reason for what he is compelled to do.

This is my dream of Education, Epictetus, but I do not know whether it can be realized. Before it can be realized, there must be a great increase in the sum of human knowledge, so that this sum may be divided. In the present state of erudition, there are not enough topics to keep the active minds of my sages safely occupied. They would always be harping on the few simple ideas of the True, the Good, and the Beautiful. They might apply these ideas, even as do the vulgar, to Cæsar himself, to whom, as thou knowest, they are not applicable.

But when knowledge has vastly increased, it may be divided skillfully, so that each sage may have some little portion over which he may exercise his wits for a lifetime, and not mingle his learning with any element dangerous to the Empire.

Thou knowest how the four elements in Nature have their likes and dislikes. The water in a closed receptacle is harmless. But when fire is applied to the vessel, the water is enraged and like a giant bursts its bonds. Knowing this antipathy between the Hot and the Moist, we learn to humor them. We use this anger of the elements to cook our food.

So I should see to it that the various knowledges of my sages were kept apart till I chose to bring them together for a purpose of my own. Their minds should be active along their several lines, and I should draw the expedient conclusions. In this way, through the influence of the learned, mankind might be made at the same time more intelligent and obedient.

I like not the story of Alexander and Diogenes. Had Alexander been as wise as he was valiant, he would not have asked condescendingly what he could do for a philosopher, and so have brought on himself the rude retort about getting out of the sunshine. Had he been a more experienced prince, he would have seated himself in the shadow of the tub and begun the conversation modestly.

" This is excellent sunshine of thine, Diogenes,

and it is greatly to thy credit to enjoy it, so that there is need of nothing beside it to make thee as happy as thy severe philosophy will allow. I come to ask thy help in matters of state. Couldst thou not teach my new subjects, whom I have deprived of their homes, to be satisfied with the sunshine which kind Nature gives to those from whom military necessity has taken all else? Perhaps when they have learned thy wisdom, they may feel that my coming among them has been for the best.

"I was about to say, when I first saw thee sitting in the sun, that if I were not Alexander I would be Diogenes. But now my ambition grows and I ask myself, why not be both? Alexander could only subjugate the world. But under Alexander-Diogenes the world would be subjugated and contented."

Diogenes would not be asked to change his manner of life. But as Alexander's man his virtues could be profitably employed.

I have written thus fully, Epictetus, because the subject is one of great importance. Whether the learned should be held as slaves, as is to some extent our present custom, may be a matter about which future ages may hold different opinions. They may have improved methods for producing that harmonious subordination of the true to the expedient which is the great necessity. Even now there are those who think it more economical to hire a sage than to own him outright. With such I have no quarrel, being content to hold my own opinion and to allow others an equal liberty.

But the all-important thing is the *status* of the thinker. Shall the man who knows be encouraged to tell all he knows, or shall his utterance be controlled by some one in authority over him?

If the thinker is all the time uttering his own thoughts, he will be a continual annoyance. He will interfere both with the pleasure and the profit of those whose right to happiness is equal to his own. There will never be an equilibrium in a society so organized. No sooner has a plan begun to work profitably than some one thinks of an improvement upon it. No sooner have men begun to accept an existing condition than some one points a way out. Thus new experiments will always be tried by restless spirits.

It is necessary, then, that intellectual force should be controlled in the interest of those who have shown their ability to rule by actually ruling, and their fitness to prosper by actually prospering.

Let one thing be made clear. It is not thought that we object to; it is only the too specific application of thought. One may admire the lightning playing among the clouds and yet cry out when the bolt strikes his own house. Cannot wisdom flash among the clouds, without destroying the cheerful house of Folly? It should be taught to keep its place.

As for thee, Epictetus, I glory in the working of thy clear mind. Think deeply, think loftily, but do not disturb the business or the pleasures of thy moral inferiors. I am thy moral inferior, I humbly acknowledge it. But I am thy legal master, and I bid thee not to disturb me.

Thou wert born to be the ornament of thy age. Thou hast a lofty soul. Meddle not, then, with things too low for thee.

Peace be with thee, Epictetus, and good sense. And let me hear no more complaints of slavery.

Epictetus the Slave to his legal owner Epaphroditus

Whether slavery, Epaphroditus, should be, to a philosopher, a matter of indifference, like heat or cold, pain and penury, and the calumny of the vulgar, is a question to which, in spite of your admonition, I must return. So far as I am merely a philosopher, your arguments have weight. I can school myself to endure the inconvenience of the outward state, while I retreat into the inner sanctuary where thought is free.

But you have imposed upon me another duty. Your ambition is that I should not only possess my soul in patience, but that I also should teach the nature of that virtue which befits free men. If I should teach only the servile virtues, I should lose all value in your eyes. You would throw me on the market for what I might fetch while you invested in more valuable human property.

The question comes to this, Is it possible for a man to be a slave and at the same time be a faithful teacher of the truth? Before we answer this question, we must consider the nature of truth. Can you, Epaphroditus, with all your wealth buy the truth, and show a clear title to it? If so, you, having a superfluity of this commodity, may send me to sell some of it in the open market.

I go to the market and cry: "Here am I, Epictetus, the slave of Epaphroditus, and I will sell you some of my master's truth. It is the truth he lives by, and he is willing to sell it cheap." Will not the free-born youths laugh as they bargain with me, "There are the cast-off moral garments of Nero's courtier Epaphroditus. Truly they seem little the worse for wear. But how did this slave come into the possession of so much truth? It looks suspicious. Perhaps he is only the receiver of stolen goods."

It is impossible for me to teach the truth in that way. No one will receive it. People are willing to receive the gold of Epaphroditus, but not his truth. Not all my skill in argument would make them believe it genuine.

The truth, Epaphroditus, is not a commodity that can thus be bought and sold; it can only be seen and obeyed. And it can only be seen and obeyed by free men. And when it is obeyed, it must be obeyed unto the uttermost. It tolerates no other master. You ask me to teach in such a way as not to interfere with your chosen way of life or with the society of which you are a part. How can I do this and still be a teacher? I might keep a true thought a close prisoner in my own mind. But the teacher does not hold his thought; he releases it. It straightway flies to another mind and urges it to action. How can you expect your lame slave to follow his freed thoughts that now have entered into minds more enterprising and courageous than his own? If I teach justice, how can I prevent some quick-witted young man from doing a just deed that may disturb the business of my master?

Should I teach what to my own mind seems false, you would then hear it said, "Epaphroditus has been fooled. His moral philosopher on whom he set so high a price has proved to be a vulgar fraud."

You ask me to teach truth, but to beware of making specific applications of it. It is as if you had commanded one to strike a light, but to prevent it from shining. It is the nature of the light to shine, and we can do nothing against nature. I do not need to point out applications of truth. Those who hear apply it.

When ardent youths come to me and I say to them, "Resist the doer of an unrighteous deed," how can I prevent some of the more intelligent and headstrong from saying, "He means that we should resist Epaphroditus"?

How can I hinder such dangerous application of my doctrine?

You ask me to teach the difference between the just and the unjust. Then I must be allowed freedom to point out the living examples of each.

Suppose that I were your charioteer and you should say, "Epictetus, drive me swiftly through the crowded streets to the Forum, and then out along the Appian Way to the sixth milestone, and returning to the city, take me to the Circus Maximus. In order that you may obey me implicitly I will blind your eyes."

I should answer, with as much respect as was possible: "My master, were you the charioteer and were you carrying me through the streets, I should submit to be blindfolded without a murmur. But if I am to be the charioteer, I must ask to be allowed to use my own eyes. I ask this free use of my own faculties, not for my own sake, but for your sake and the chariot's."

The teacher is the charioteer along the crowded ways where Truth and Falsehood jostle. He must be able to see and choose the right way. This is a freeman's work and to entrust it to a slave is to invite disaster. Therefore, Epaphroditus, if you determine that I am to remain your slave, give me a task which a slave can properly perform.

THE CHARM OF SEVENTEENTH-CENTURY PROSE

PROSE is what all of us write when we are able to write nothing else. Poetry has charm, at least in the mind of the poet, or he would not write it. But Prose is the Cinderella of literature and must mind the pots and kettles while her proud sisters go to the ball.

But now and then the Fairy Godmother appears, and Cinderella has her fling. She has for a little time, "beauty for ashes, the garment of praise for the spirit of heaviness." Just as there are periods when genius expresses itself in a lyric or dramatic form, so there are periods when it expresses itself in narrative or even didactic prose.

The sixteenth century was an age favorable to poetry. Its spirit was one of romantic expectation. All sorts of dazzling possibilities opened up to the excited imagination. Men found the ordinary speech inadequate.

Stout Sir Thomas Stuckley of Ilfracombe, when he talked with Queen Elizabeth about his plantation in Florida, began to rhapsodize. He would not exchange his prospects in Florida for anything that could be offered him in the courts of Europe.

"I hope," said the Queen, "I may hear from you when you are seated in your principality."

"I will write unto you," quoth Stuckley.

"In what language?" said the Queen.

"In the language of princes," said Stuckley: "To our dear sister."

When merchant adventurers adopted the language of princes, they would prefer the "Faerie Queene" to any prosaic textbook on Ethics. There was the exhilaration which comes when great revolutionary ideas are in the air, which have not yet been reduced to inconvenient action. Young men dreamed dreams and old men saw visions, and left the next generation to pay the bills.

When the spacious times of great Elizabeth had passed into history, the bills for the sixteenth-century improvements in Civilization became due. The theory of civil and religious liberty had been adopted, but now the practical consequences must be considered. Who was to pay for the new freedom?

Now, when men begin to talk about ways and means to make both ends meet, they are more apt to use prose than poetry. They are likely also to lose their tempers. After the triumph of Protestantism in England there came the period of internal strife — Parliament against the King, Churchman against Puritan, and every one against that "world-hating and world-hated beast the haggard Anabaptist." Law-abiding citizens were appalled at the new broods of anarchists. Whether they were called Ranters, or Quakers, or Root-and-Branch men, or Fifth Monarchy men, they pestered quiet people, and interfered with business. They perpetuated the social unrest. There's one phrase that continually occurs — "these are distracted times."

To persons of a quiet habit it seemed to mark the breaking-up of Civilization. Churches were ruined, property rights ignored, clergy deprived of their livings, the hereditary aristocracy degraded from its place of power, the Constitution overthrown, and at last the anointed King tried and executed as a common traitor.

And yet it was in this period of bitter civil war that we have one of the flowering times of English literature. And what is more remarkable is, that it is to this period of strife that we go back to find health and a sense of leisure. It was the age of George Herbert and Izaak Walton, of Thomas Fuller, of Jeremy Taylor, of John Milton, of Clarendon and John Bunyan.

If I were to indicate the chief characteristic of these men I should say that it was their ability to give an uncommon expression to common sense. Now, while in practical life common sense is looked upon as a virtue, in the arts it is often considered to be the sum of all villainies. For it is taken as but another name for the irremediably commonplace.

Horace Walpole tells us how one day he met Hogarth who insisted on talking at great length on his history of English painting. "The reason," said Hogarth, "why we English do not paint better is because we have too much common sense." It was before the Cubists had shown to what heights painting could rise when the inhibitions of common sense were completely removed.

But the criticism was suggestive. Poetry suffers from too much common sense. Its wings are clipped and it cannot soar. Music is of the same nature. Grand opera would be impossible if the tenor in expressing his affection for his ladylove took counsel of his common sense. But prose does not need to soar. It is pedestrian in its habit. It is at its best with its feet on the solid earth. But with his feet upon the ground a man may shuffle along, or limp and totter, or he may dawdle on the path or walk mincingly till we lose all interest in his uncertain progression. Or, on the other hand, he may walk with a firm, confident stride, as one who knows where he is going and who enjoys the wholesome exercise. Such a pedestrian would not exchange a stout pair of legs for any ordinary kind of wings. And there is a prose which for power to stir us is surpassed only by the rarest kind of poetry.

The characteristic of the great prose-writers of the seventeenth century was huge, heroic common sense. It was the common sense of middle-aged gentlemen, not in slippered ease, but in fighting trim, and carrying the very least amount of adipose tissue.

Usually common sense arrives at that period when the spirit of adventure is dead. It takes the form of good-humored cynicism. The prudential virtues are treated as a residuum after the tumults of youth have subsided. So in the gulches of the Far West, below some old mining camp where the gambling spirit once ran high, you may see the patient, unemotional Chinaman working over the tailings. He gets a sufficient living out of what in the wasteful days had been allowed to run through the sluices.

There is another kind of prudence. It is active, not passive. It is forward-looking, not reminiscent. It is a practitioner of preventive medicine for the body politic.

> Think not that Prudence dwells in dark abodes ;
> She scans the Future with the eye of gods.

The ideal is that of one who, in Miltonic phrase, is " a skillful considerer of human things."

Amid the tumults of the seventeenth century, there arose an unusual number of skillful considerers of human things. Some of them were radicals, some of them conservatives. Some fought for the King and some for the Parliament, but they had certain qualities in common. Theirs was the large utterance of men who were dealing with big questions. They had no time for hair-splitting; there was a manly grasp of principles, and acceptance of responsibilities, as of those to whom words and deeds corresponded. They were all the time dealing with conduct. Men took up the pen as they would take up the sword, for a worthy cause. How far from the temper which we are accustomed to call literary is Milton's description of the way in which a man fits himself for authorship: "When a man writes to the world, he summons up all his reason and deliberation to assist him, he searches, meditates, is industrious and likely consults and confers with his judicious friends, after all which done he takes himself to be informed in what he writes, as well as any that writ before him." This is "the most consummate act of his fidelity and ripeness."

In that age of exuberant pamphleting, not all that was written and printed would stand that test — certainly not all of Milton's tracts for the times. But out of the mass of passionate and even scurrilous invective there emerges a remarkable literature, in which common sense is transfigured and appears as something romantic. Milton has it, so has Jeremy Taylor, and so has John Bunyan. You feel that you are in the presence of persons who have the valor not of ignorance but of experience.

How characteristic is Jeremy Taylor's praise of manly virtue: " Our virtues are but the seed when the Grace of God comes upon us first, but this grace must be thrown into broken furrows, and must twice feel the cold and twice feel the heat, and be softened with storms and showers, and then it will arise into fruitfulness and harvests. . . . Fathers because they design to have their children wise and valiant, apt for counsel or for arms, send them to severe governments and tie them to study, to hard labor. They rejoice when the bold boy strikes a lion with his hunting spear, and shrinks not when the beast comes to affright his early courage. Softness is for slaves, for minstrels, for useless persons, for the fair ox. But the man that designs his son for noble employments loves to see him pale with study, or panting with labor, hardened with sufferance, or eminent by dangers. And so God dresses us for Heaven."

The same appeal to disciplined courage which is the note in England is felt in New England. A great part of the fame of the Plymouth and Massachusetts Bay colonists comes from the fact that they were their own historians and realized the ideal significance of their own doings. No orator on Forefathers' Day can do better than take his text from some great utterance of Governor Bradford: "They had a great hope and inward zeal of laying some good foundation." The whole story of the men of the Mayflower, their inner and their outward lives, is in that pregnant sentence. We read it as Holy Writ, and the History of Freedom in America is the commentary.

Or we linger over that other text, which follows the list of discouragements to the new undertakings: " It was answered that all great and honorable actions are accompanied with great difficulties and must be both enterprised and overcome by answerable courages."

Even in the narrative of the most ordinary event there is an arresting quality. Governor Winthrop had been guilty of the indiscretion of moving his house from Cambridge; for this he was called to account by the fiery Dudley. But how admirable is the description of the quarrel that ensued: "The deputy began to be in a passion and told the Governor that if he were so round, he would be round also. So the deputy rose in a great fury and passion, and the Governor grew very hot also. And they both fell into a fury of bitterness. But by the mediation of the mediators they were soon pacified. . . . So the meeting breaking up without any other consideration but the commending of the success of it by prayer to the Lord, the Governor brought the deputy onward of his way, and every man went to his own home."

That is only a straightforward narrative of one of the commonest incidents of local politics. Yet it is told in such a way that it is invested with an atmosphere of moral dignity. They were angry and sinned not, — at least they did not sin against the canons of good literature.

There was a peculiar flavor to the speech of

the men of that period which we recognize in
their most casual talk. We listen to the remark
of King James I at a dinner table: "He must
have been a very valiant man who first adven-
tured upon the eating of an oyster." We have
all had that thought, but we could not express
it in that way.

The fact is that the men of that generation had
a great advantage over us in the material with
which they worked. The builder in concrete con-
struction is careful in his specifications to demand not only a good quality of Portland cement
but also a sufficiency of sharp sand. Not only
must there be something that binds, but there
must be material that can be bound.

So in our speech. There is a fluency not to
say fluidity in our present language which makes
for easy writing but does not produce structural
strength. The sentence is flowing or at best a
sticky mass that does not "set." The words
themselves are not clean and sharp. They have
no edge. Words that have been used in so many
senses that their original significance has been
forgotten come at length to form only a verbal
quicksand.

The older writers had at their command an abundance of clean, sharp words. It mattered little whether the words were Anglo-Saxon or Latin in their origin. The important thing was that their primary meanings were in the minds of both speakers and listeners. The word and the thing had not only analogy but an identity. It was said of Sir Walter Raleigh, "He seemed to be born to be that only which he went about." When such men spoke, their words fitted their mood. Their utterance was individual, as much their own as their sword thrusts.

Let us compare two forms of speech. Here is a sentence from a recent novel: "As he went downstairs he halted at the landing, his hand going to his forehead, a reflex motion significant of a final attempt to achieve the hitherto unattainable feat of imagining her to be his wife." There is something of self-conscious modernity in this sentence. The accepted lover is a bundle of hesitancies. In the attempt to psychologize over his emotions, we are in doubt whether he will get downstairs or not; we certainly do not see him do it. There is nothing suggested but a series of reflex actions which will in all human probability come to nothing.

Now turn to Izaak Walton: "My honest scholar, it is now past five of the clock. We will fish till nine and then go to breakfast. Go you to yonder sycamore tree and hide your bottle of drink under the hollow root of it, for about that time and in that place we will make a brave breakfast with a piece of powdered beef and a radish or two, which I have in my fish bag. We shall, I warrant you, make a good, honest, wholesome, hungry breakfast. And I will then give you direction for the making and using of your flies."

What is the difference? There is a difference not only in the arrangement of the sentences, but in the nature of the words. In one case the words are listless and indifferent. They look as if they had been up late at night and had lost interest in life. They are self-conscious, as if they had just come out of the psychology book and were sorry that they had left it.

In the other case the words have the dew of the morning upon them. They are brisk and cheery. They stand erect and look you in the eye. They are glad to be alive. It is only a piece of dried beef and a radish or two that is promised, but it is a brave breakfast, a good, honest, wholesome, hungry breakfast. We are sure of that. The very words make us hungry.

"It's only a way of putting things, a mere trick of language," do you say? But language is not a trick, it is an expression of personality. Find out a man's natural and habitual way of expressing himself and you find out a great deal about the man. We talk about expressing a thought in different language, but are you sure that in your paraphrase you have expressed all the thought — or if the thought, have you also expressed the feeling?

In the card catalogue of the Boston Library there is the title of a book published about a hundred years ago. It is "An Attempt to translate the prophetic part of the Apocalypse of St. John into familiar language, by divesting it of the metaphors in which it is involved." My curiosity was not sufficient to lead me to take out the book, but I should imagine that it would not be very much like the Apocalypse.

The attempt to treat literary style apart from

the personality of which it is the expression leads us unto those regions of scholarship which belong to the permanently arid belt. However keen the analysis, it does not reveal the secret of charm or of force.

The true lover of literature is discovered by the simple test which King Solomon found so efficacious when the two women claimed each for herself the living child. The critic with Solomonic gravity lifts his sword to cleave asunder the living work of genius. " I will divide the word from the thought. I will give to one the literary form and to the other the actual meaning of this passage." Then the literal-minded student of literature says, "Divide it." But the loving reader cries, " Not so, my Lord. Give her the living child, and in no wise slay it." It all depends, of course, on the kind of literature which we have in mind, whether it is the kind that lives, or is the kind that is merely put together.

Bergson in his "Creative Evolution" points out the difference between a vital process and a manufacture. The manufacturer finds in his product exactly what he put into it. The pieces are put together and form a complete whole. But life has an explosive quality about it, and each bit into which it explodes has power to reproduce itself, and is influenced by a new set of circumstances. Therefore, "Life in evolving sows itself in an unforeseeable variety of form."

Now the same thing is true in literary history. There are writers who are careful craftsmen. Their manufactured works are admirably done. They use words which express their thoughts with absolute precision. It is a case where we find precisely what the manufacturer put into it. And yet though we read and admire them, we find it difficult to remember them. The reason of this is that we are very self-centered creatures, and we can't remember what other people have thought nearly so well as we can what we have been thinking ourselves.

It is here that real genius for expression comes in. Some one, in an unforgettable sentence, drops a thought into our mind. Henceforth it is not his but ours. He was but the sower going forth to sow; but our minds form the field, and the harvest is ours. There are books which have this germinating power. No matter what the original writer thought, their great value is in what they cause us to think. "Words that are simple," said the Chinese sage, "but whose meanings are far-reaching, are good words." There are inner meanings, suggestions and universal applications. The Christian Apostle urges us to "provoke one another to good works." So there are books which do not so much furnish us with thoughts as provoke us to good thinking. In such provocation the form is very essential.

Of this provocative quality, the Bible is the supreme example. An old writer says of it, "Where the surface doth not laugh with corn, the heart thereof within is merry with mines." It provokes in us a curiosity which leads us to dig for hidden treasure.

But even the Bible has gained immensely in its power over English-speaking people by the fact that it was translated at a period when the language was peculiarly vital, and the words had not lost their explosive power.

In Scripture texts it is very difficult to change the language without a sense of impoverishment. Any one can test this for himself by comparing the King James Version with the so-called Twentieth Century Version, whose translators state their principle to be to "exclude all words and phrases not used in current English." This version, while it has a value of its own, may serve as a criticism of current English.

Read the story of the Nativity. "When Herod the King had heard these things he was troubled and all Jerusalem with him." This is the simplest form of narrative, but it is vital. Read it in any time of popular commotion and vague unrest. How the words come back as we see the troubled rulers and the troubled city. It is a text which expresses the feeling which comes in a great civic crisis.

But suppose the preacher were compelled to take his text from the Twentieth Century Version. "When King Herod heard the news he was much troubled and his anxiety was shared by the whole of Jerusalem." Even the person least sensitive to literary charm must feel that something had happened to the text. "A city set upon a hill cannot be hid." These words kindle thought. The Twentieth Century Version reads, "It is impossible for a town that stands on a hill to escape notice." These words are a verbal wet blanket.

In this praise of the seventeenth-century prose I do not mean to cast discredit on our own time. We have many excellent writers who have contributed to the wealth of our literature.

But for our health's sake it is well now and then to escape from our contemporaries and enjoy the companionship of men of another generation. This is not to say that the former times are better than these, but they were different. To those who need a change the seventeenth century may be recommended as a health resort.

Every age has its literary fashions and the critics who sit in high places and tell us what we ought to admire and why. But in spite of their excellent reasons we often fret under their restrictions.

But there is no reason whatever why we should submit to the tyranny of the contemporaneous. Literature cannot be subject to monopoly. The reader as the ultimate consumer can snap his fingers at both the middleman and the producers. His mind is an open port. Ships from all centuries can land their cargoes and no one can prevent them. If he does not find what he likes in one age, he can trade with another.

To those who have troubles enough of their own to make them value literature as a means of reinvigoration, the seventeenth century may be heartily recommended. There may be found good air and good exercise in the companionship of men of robust intelligence and of unfailing common sense. They had their faults, but they never mistook neurasthenia for genius.

It is a literature produced, not by specialists or dreamers or by sophisticated spectators, but by men of action of whom it could be said as it was said of Sir Henry Wotton: "He did ever love to join with business study and trial of natural experiments."

Here we may find scholars who left "the still air of delightful studies" to engage in the strenuous politics of the day. Here we may find honest gentlemen who, when the tide of fortune was against them, learned to find content by the side of quiet streams.

"Let me tell you," says Izaak Walton, "that there be many that have forty times our estates who would give the greater part of it to be healthful and cheerful like us, who with the expense of a little money have eat and drunk and laughed and angled and sung, and slept securely and rose next day and cast away care and laughed and angled again."

Or we may sit at table with Selden and hear him discourse wisely and wittily about the constitution and laws.

Or we may listen to that wise physician Sir Thomas Browne: "I thank God with joy, I was never afraid of hell, nor grew pale at the mention of that place. I fear God, but I am not afraid of him. I can hardly think any one was scared into heaven. They go the fairest way to heaven that would serve God without a hell."

Not so did John Bunyan feel. He was horribly afraid of hell. But what of it? Mr. Honest trudges on the difficult road. He has an honest fear, but he has an honest courage also, and on the road can eat as brave a breakfast as any angler of them all.

"How fares it in your pilgrimage?" asks Mr. Contrite. "It happens to us as it happeneth to all wayfaring men, sometimes our way is clean, sometimes foul, sometimes up hill, sometimes down. The wind is not always at our backs nor is every one a friend whom we meet by the way. We have met some notable rubs already, and what is yet before we know not, but for the most part we find it true that has been talked of old, that a good man must suffer trouble."

As we listen to his talk we agree with Mr. Great Heart as he cries, "Well said, Father Honest; by this I know that thou art a cock of the right kind, for thou hast said the truth."

Whatever their politics or religion we feel that these were men of the right kind, and we are glad that they wrote books.

And if it should happen that there should be a strike among living authors and no new books should be produced for a year and a day, we should not be discouraged. We should call in

these sturdy strike-breakers from the seventeenth
century. With their aid we should, in Bunyan's
pithy phrase, make "a pretty good shift to wag
along."

THOMAS FULLER AND HIS
"WORTHIES"

FEBRUARY 23, 1661 (Lord's Day). My cold being increased, I staid at home all day pleasing myself in my dining-room, now graced with pictures, and reading of Dr. Fuller's Worthys. So I spent the day. . . . I reckon myself as happy as any man in the world, for which God be praised."

It was indeed a day for comfortable thoughts. It was Sunday, and Pepys could, without self-reproach, and indeed with a real sense of virtue, abstain from worldly business. And Pepys had a cold and need not go to church where in those days he was quite often irritated by the parsons. And here was Fuller's "Worthies of England," only recently published and waiting to be read.

No, it was not the kind of book that insisted on being read. Its invitation was of a different kind. It was not made to be read. It was rather to be opened here and there, and dipped into, and tasted. Then the process could be repeated as long as one was so disposed. It was just the thing for a gentleman who was kept in all Sunday with a cold.

Pepys had seen the book a short time before in a book-stall and dipped into it. But then he had an ulterior purpose. He wanted to see if any of his ancestors were mentioned in the "Worthies of England." Unfortunately, he could find no one of the name of Pepys in those hospitable pages. Being a sensible person he did n't blame Fuller, but drew the rational conclusion that the family was not as considerable as he had supposed.

But now on this fortunate Sunday he had nothing to do but to make acquaintance with some of the gentlemen of England who attracted his attention. No wonder that he had a good time. It was a kind of refreshment with which he was familiar. After a dull day in the office he writes: "To the Privy Seale where I signed a deadly number of pardons which do trouble me to get nothing by. I fell a reading Fuller's History of Abbys." Since that day there have

been many who have found refreshment in the
same source. Dear to Charles Lamb was the
humor of Thomas Fuller. Says Lamb, " Fuller's
way of telling a story, for its eager liveliness and
running commentary of the narrator happily
blended with the narration, is perhaps un-
equalled.' Many have taken in hand, as did
Lamb himself, to make collections of the " Wit
and Humor of Thomas Fuller." But these ex-
cerpts fail to do justice to one whom Coleridge
declared to be " the most sensible and the least
prejudiced great man of an age that boasted a
galaxy of great men."

For while Fuller's wit flashed in sentences,
his wisdom required the bulky volumes which
contain his works. For Fuller was one of the
most voluminous as well as one of the most
popular writers of his time. The very bulk of
his writing adds to the impression of abounding
good humor. He diffuses around the reader a
soothing atmosphere of unlimited leisure. He
has power to exorcise the foul fiends Hurry and
Worry.

And yet this most leisurely of writers not only
lived through the turmoils of the English civil

wars, but took an active part in them. He was a clergyman of the Church of England, a Royalist by conviction, a chaplain of the King, living much in camps, and surrounded by bitter partisans. He took sides heartily, and for a good part of his life he was on the losing side.

But having made all the personal sacrifices necessary to show his loyalty, Fuller drew the line beyond which he would not go. He would not sacrifice his sanity and good temper even for the King and the Church.

The times were out of joint, but he refused to exaggerate the evils of the day. "Many things in England are out of joint for the present and a strange confusion there is in Church and State, but let this comfort us that it is a confusion in tendency to order." Had Fuller been a professor of History, writing two centuries after, he could not have better summed up the situation.

Having come to this philosophic conclusion concerning the times Fuller proceeded to make the best of the circumstances as they developed. He knew he was to be jolted over abominable roads of progress at a rate that was disagreeable to him, but fortunately his mind was furnished with a shock-absorber. Humor was a solace at a time when politics was a nightmare. Writing of one Bishop Young at the beginning of the civil wars, he says, "I heard him preach from the text — 'The waters are risen, O God, the waters are risen.' Whereupon he complained of the invasions of popular violence in Church and State. The Bishop was sadly sensible of those inundations and yet he safely waded through."

How admirably English that was. There was no use denying that fact that the waters were risen. But what of it? A sensible clergyman would tuck up his cassock and wade through. It was in this good-humored way that Fuller passed through the days of Puritan ascendancy.

At the beginning of the troubles he published a little volume of homilies entitled, "Good Thoughts for Bad Times." A few years after there followed, "Good Thoughts for Worse Times," and when the cause of the King began to mend, "Mixed Contemplations for Better Times." It was in mixed contemplation that Fuller excelled.

He indicates his position in regard to many of the controversies of his time. "There dwelt not long since a devout but ignorant papist in Spain. Every morning bending his knees and lifting his eyes to heaven he would repeat the alphabet. And now he said; O good God put these letters together to spell syllables and to make such sense as may be to thy glory and my good. . . . In these distracted times I fall to the poor pious man's prayer A. B. C. D. etc."

As to the main question to be decided Fuller's ideas were clear enough, but when it came to the particular measures over which his contemporaries contended, he insisted on a suspense of judgment.

As for the zealous cries for more liberty, he thought the age was sufficiently supplied with that commodity. "It were liberty enough if for the next seven years all sermons were obliged to keep residence on the text, 'Love one another.' . . ." Too many nowadays are like Pharaoh's magicians who could conjure up with their charms new frogs, but could not drive away the frogs that were there before.

Turn from the pamphlets of the day with their

fierce invective to Fuller's little homily on the Psalms. We suddenly seem to have entered a haven of reasonableness.

"Sometimes I have disputed with myself which was the most guilty, David who said in his haste all men are liars, or that wicked man who sat and spoke against his brother and slandered his mother's son. David seems the greater offender, for mankind might have an action of defamation against him. Yea, he might be challenged for giving all men the lie. But mark: David was in haste, he spoke as it were *in transitu*, when he was passing, or rather posting by; or if you please it was not David, but David's haste that rashly vented the words. Whereas the other *sat*, a solemn, serious, premeditate posture. Now to say sat carries with it the countenance of a judicial proceeding, as if he made a session or bench business thereof. Lord pardon my cursory and preserve me from sedentary sins."

Fuller was too much a man of his own time to avoid controversy. For a theologian to have declined to enter the lists against his foeman would be as unpardonable as for an officer to decline a challenge to a duel. He must yield to the imperious custom and vindicate his honor.

Fuller's "Appeal of Injured Innocence," in answer to his adversary Dr. Heylin, is as lengthy and circumstantial as the seventeenth-century code required. It is as voluminous as if the reader had nothing to do but sit listening to the quarrels of the authors. Everything which Dr. Heylin has asserted, Dr. Fuller denies. Nothing could be more complete in form. Then, when we come to the end we see the warlike theological mask fall off and the round, smiling face of Tom Fuller reveals itself.

"You know full well, sir, how in heraldry *two lioncels rampant endorsed* are said to be the emblem of two valiant men keeping an appointment, meeting in the field but either forbidden by the King to fight or departing on terms of equality agreed upon betwixt themselves. Whereupon turning back to back, neither conquerors nor conquered, they depart their several ways (their stout stomachs not suffering both to go the same way) lest it be counted an injury for one to precede the other. In a like manner I know you disdain to allow me to be your equal in this controversy, and I will not allow you to be my superior. To prevent future trouble let it be a drawn battle, and let both of us abound in our own sense, severally persuaded in the truth of what we have written. Thus parting and going out, back to back, I hope we may meet in Heaven, face to face. In order whereunto, God willing, I will give you a meeting where you shall be pleased to appoint, that we who have tilted pens may shake hands together." He signs himself, "A lover of your parts and an honorour of your person."

It was not thus that the men of the seventeenth century usually carried on their controversies. Fuller was a Royalist, but the most zealous Parliament man could not apply to him the common term of reproach for his party — "malignant." He had, as he said of another, "a broad-chested soul, favorable to such as differed with him."

We take up a little volume of sermons published in 1656, and linger over the dedicatory epistle: "To my worthy friends in St. Bridgets Parish in London, Jacob when sending his sons into Egypt advised them to carry to the Governor there a little balm, a little honey, spices and myrrh, nuts and almonds. . . . The quantity a little of each. To carry much would have been less acceptable."

Fuller was a peace-lover, but he was not a thoroughgoing pacifist. Much as he desired that all good people in England should keep strict residence in the text, "Love one another," he saw that they were not likely to do it till they had exchanged a few more stout blows. They were not for the present in the mood to accept much in the way of good-will. But at least he could do his bit and in wartime prepare for the inevitable peace. While the other parsons were smiting the Amalekites, he could in the midst of the distracted times bring to his friends a little honey, spices, and myrrh. No one knew better than Fuller that "to carry much would have been less acceptable."

He was under no illusions. He was well aware that good temper toward his adversaries would bring upon him the charge of lukewarmness toward his friends. It would be difficult to keep close to his own party. But he comforted himself with the thought that he was like a man in the crowded fair. If, instead of nervously running about to find his friends, he took a stand in a central place, they would be likely to come his way at least once during the day.

While he was aware that his own gifts did not lie in the direction of invective, he did not object to explosions of holy wrath on fit occasions, and he writes admiringly of that excellent clergyman William Perkins, "He could pronounce the word damn with such emphasis as left a doleful echo in the hearer's mind a long time after." What he objected to was the type of man, too common in his day, who in the name of truth renounced brotherly kindness. "He was made all teeth and tongue biting whatever he touched, and it bled whenever it bit."

It was in the times of the greatest distraction, when Fuller's own livelihood was most precarious that he wrote the two masterpieces of leisure, "The Worthies of England" and "The Church History of Britain," books which seem to be written by one who had all the time in the world at his disposal. Fuller's "Church History" was written as no church history had been written before or since. It has no natural beginning or end. There is no logical sequence; no hint of development in doctrine or policy. For all Fuller cares the centuries might have been reversed and the story told backwards.

The impression that we get is that the Church of England had always been there and had always been essentially the same. It was a part of the landscape. It was connected with the county families. It was entwined with all that was most attractive in English life. Indeed, Fuller is not so much interested in the Church as in the people who belonged to it. He stops to tell us about their coats of arms because he thinks we might like to know about them.

It is such a rambling commentary as might be given us by a genial dean of a cathedral, who takes us about telling us of the knights and ladies whose monuments we see. They lived long ago, but their descendants are still in possession of the old estates. Moreover, Fuller's leisurely ramble through the centuries is interrupted by the claims of hospitality. He was living precariously and was entertained by one Royalist gentleman after another. It occurred to him that it would be a waste of good literary material to dedicate his whole history to a single benefactor leaving the others unacknowledged. So he conceived the idea of dedicating each chapter of his "Church History" to a different patron. It thus happens that the Church of England is often forgotten for whole pages while we listen to the praises of Fuller's many friends. But it is all pleasant and familiar, and deepens the impression that the Church of England is essentially a family affair and has its roots in the family affections.

Even in his description of the great revolutionary events Fuller retains the intimate tone of one who is in a little circle of friends. There is no attempt at the impartial dignity of history. If he tells what happens, he takes it for granted that we should like to know what he thinks about it.

Charles Lamb might have written the account of what followed on the dissolution of the monasteries: —

"As the old clothes dealers of Long Lane when they buy an old suit buy the linings together with the outside, so those that bought the buildings of the Monasteries had also the libraries conveyed to them. The curious brasses and clasps were the baits of covetousness, and many excellent old authors were left naked. Some ancient manuscripts were sold to grocers and soap sellers, some to scour candlesticks, some to rub boots, and whole ships full sent abroad to undoing of foreign nations.

"What beautiful bibles, rare fathers, subtle schoolmen, useful historians, all massacred together. Holy divinity was profaned, physic itself hurt, and the history of former time received a dangerous wound, whereof it halts to this day, and without hope of a perfect cure must go a cripple to the grave.

"Some will say that I herein discover a harking after the onions and flesh pots of Egypt. To such I protest that I have not the least inclination to monkery. But enough. As for these back-friends of learning whom I have jogged in my discourse, we will let them alone to be settled in the lees of their own ignorance, praying God that never a good library be left to their disposal."

One may say that this is no way to write history. Fuller would answer that it was his way.

"We read of King Ahasuerus that having his head troubled with much business and finding himself so indisposed that he could not sleep, he caused the records to be brought in to him hoping thereby to deceive the tediousness of the time, and that the pleasant passages in the chronicles would either invite slumber or enable him to bear waking with less molestation. We live in a troublesome age and he needs to have a soft bed who can sleep nowadays amidst so much loud noise and many impetuous rumors. Wherefore it seemeth to me both a safe and cheap receipt to procure quiet and repose to the mind that complains of want of rest to prescribe the reading of History. Great is the pleasure and profit thereof."

In following his own humor Fuller may have transgressed many of the conventions of formal history for which he finds ready pardon.

Our mining law declares that "A man is entitled to his vein and all its dips, spurs, and angles, although it may depart so far from the perpendicular as to pass the side lines of the location within the plane of the lines extended."

Fuller would have paid no attention to the

perpendicular lines limiting his subject and dividing the "Church History of Britain" from other interesting objects of thought. The lover of Fuller's vein is content to follow it through all its dips and spurs and angles, without regard to the side lines of the location. If we do not find what we expected, we find something else which is of more value.

And after all, I am not sure but that Fuller may have given us an essential truth which the more systematic historians often overlook.

He gives the same impression which one gets when he lingers in rural England. The village church with its ancient yew tree, the church-yard where the generations lie, the rectory hard by, the cathedral and its close; these do not speak of events to be narrated. They speak of something permanent; they are deep-rooted in the English earth; they represent a life mellow and fruitful. The successive generations might well be thought of as contemporaneous, living as they do in an environment that has been so constant. This is only one aspect of history, but it is an important one, and one that is often ignored.

It is a far cry from Fuller's "Worthies of England" to the "Spoon River Anthology," but the fundamental idea of the two works is the same. It occurred to our present-day anthologist to take the worthies and the unworthies of an American village and sum up their characteristics with all the brevity and more than the veracity which we associate with the epitaph. Fuller had the advantage of having all England for his province and also the advantage of liking most of his worthies.

He takes England by counties. He introduces us to the people that have been most noteworthy. They are not confined to any one generation. The "Worthies" are Catholic or Protestant, they are country gentlemen, statesmen, physicians, privateers, clergymen, lawyers. Some of them have great names in history, others live now only in these pages. But Fuller manages in a sentence or two to make us see what manner of persons they were. Each little portrait has an unmistakable individuality.

I know nothing of Bishop Foliot but what Fuller tells us, but I feel remarkably well acquainted with him: "He was observed when a common brother to inveigh against the prior; when prior he inveighed against the abbot; when abbot against the pride and laziness of the bishop. When he was a bishop, all was well. Foliot's mouth when full was silent."

As Foliot represents a certain kind of reformer, so Fuller gives us a sketch of a certain kind of philanthropist: "I have observed some in the Church cast in a sixpence with such ostentation that it rebounded from the bottom and rung against both sides of the basin — so that the same piece of silver was alms and the trumpet."

Of one Allyn he writes: "He made friends of his unrighteous mammon building therewith a fair college at Dulwich, for the relief of the poor people. Some, I confess, count it built on a foundered foundation, seeing in a spiritual sense none is good and lawful money save what is honestly gotten. But perchance some who condemn master Allyn have as bad a shilling in the bottom of their purses, if search were made in them."

Here we have an example of Fuller's capacity for mixed contemplation. He has a shrewd suspicion of tainted money, but his common sense makes him perceive that it is not a simple matter to prevent its being put to good uses. He rejoices in the fair college at Dulwich in spite of the question in regard to Master Allyn.

What sound philosophy is put into the sentence which tells of the mediæval schoolman John Baconthorpe: "He groped after more light than he saw; he saw more than he durst speak of; and he spoke of more than he was thanked for by those of his superstitious order."

He stood in strong contrast to that Saxon king known as Ethelred the Unready: "The clock of his consultations was always set some hours too late, vainly striving with much industry to redress what a little providence might have prevented. Now when this unready king met with the Danes, his ever ready enemies, no wonder if lamentable was the event thereof."

It is to Fuller that we owe the picture of the "wit combats" between Shakespeare and Ben Jonson compared to a battle between a Spanish galleon and an English man-of-war. "Master Jonson like the former was built far higher in learning, solid but slow in performance. Shakespeare, with the English man-of-war, lesser in bulk but lighter in starting, could turn with all tides, tack about, and take advantage of all winds."

What delights us in "The Worthies of England" is to find that Shakespeare and the great men whose names are familiar are not set apart but take their places with the multitude of men of the same breed. We are made to feel that men of strong character and fine gifts were too common in England to be made much of. Fame seems almost a vulgarity.

Sometimes Fuller comes across a worthy for whom he can do nothing but snatch his name from oblivion.

He says of Robert Vanite: "This put me to blushing that one so eminent in himself should be obscure to me. But all my industry could not retrieve the valiant knight, so that he seems to me akin to those spirits who appear but once and then vanish away."

There are more heroic figures in the seventeenth century than the Royalist parson whom his contemporaries called "Tom Fuller," and whom those who came after quoted as "Old Thomas Fuller." "Old" was an adjective never

appropriate to him save as a term of affectionate familiarity.

But if heroism consists in being faithful to
one's own ideals rather than to those imposed
by one's contemporaries I am not sure but that he
deserved the title "heroic." When men are making a religion of hating one another, it requires
some courage to follow one's own generous
inclination. Sanity may in time of fanaticism be
lifted to heroic proportions. To love one's enemies, or rather to assent to the proposition that
it is virtuous to love one's enemies, is often easier
than to treat them as ordinary human beings
who are very troublesome at present, but who
may be better by and by. This was Fuller's habitual attitude. In pleading for moderation he was
careful to distinguish it from lukewarmness.
The moderate men are commonly attacked by
both extreme parties. But what of it? "As the
moderate man's temporal hopes are not great,
so his fears are the less. He fears not to have
the splinters of his party when it breaks fly into
his eyes, or to be buried under the ruins of his
side, if suppressed. He never pinned his religion
on any man's sleeve."

He was fortunate in his life, making friends in adversity, and giving cheer to those who sadly needed it. And death came in time to prevent a catastrophe which might have obscured for us that which is most distinctive.

For Charles the Second was about to make him a bishop. This would have been a calamity. Thomas Fuller would have made a very poor bishop.

A LITERARY CLINIC

THE other day, on going by my friend
Bagster's church, I saw a new sign over
the vestry : —

"Bibliopathic Institute. Book Treatment by
Competent Specialists. Dr. Bagster meets patients by appointment. Free Clinic 2–4 P.M.
Out-patients looked after in their homes by
members of the Social Service Department.
Young People's Lend-a-Thought Club every
Sunday evening at 7.30. Tired Business Men
in classes. Tired Business Men's tired wives
given individual treatment. Tired mothers who
are reading for health may leave their children
in the Day Nursery."

It had been several years since I had seen
Bagster. At that time he had been recuperating
after excessive and too widely diffused efforts
for the public good. Indeed, the variety of his
efforts for the public good had been too much

for him. Nothing human was foreign to Bagster. All sorts of ideas flocked from the ends of the earth and claimed citizenship in his mind. No matter how foreign the idea might be, it was never interned as an alien enemy. The result was he had suffered from the excessive immigration of ideas that were not easily assimilated by the native stock. I have sometimes thought that it might have been better if he had not allowed these aliens a controlling influence till they had taken out their first naturalization papers. But that was not Bagster's way.

Dropping into what once was known as the vestry of the church, but which is now the office of the Institute, I found a row of patients sitting with an air of expectant resignation. A business-like young woman attempted to put my name on an appointment card. I mumbled an excuse to the effect that I was a friend of the doctor and wished to remain so, and therefore would not call during office-hours.

The next day I was fortunate enough to find Bagster in one of his rare periods of leisure and to hear from his own lips an account of his new enterprise.

"You know," he said, "I was unfortunate enough to be out of health several years ago, at the time when the ministers began to go into Psychotherapy. I liked the idea and would have gone into it too, but I had to let my mind lie fallow for a while. It seemed too bad not to have a clinic. We ought all to be healthier than we are, and if we could get the right thoughts and hold on to them, we should get rid of a good many ills. Even the M.D.'s admit that. I read up on the subject and started in to practice as soon as I got back. For a while, everything went well. When a patient came I would suggest to him a thought which he should hold for the benefit of his soul and body."

"What was the difficulty with the treatment?"

"The fact is," said Bagster, "I ran out of thoughts. It's all very well to say, 'Hold a thought.' But what if there is n't anything you can get a grip on? You know the law of the association of ideas. That's where the trouble lies. An idea will appear to be perfectly reliable, and you think you know just where to find it. But it falls in with idle associates and plays truant. When you want it, it isn't there. And there are a lot of solid thoughts that have been knocking about in the minds of everybody till their edges are worn off. You can't hold them. A thought to be held must be interesting. When I read that in the Psychology, I was staggered.

"To be interesting, a thought must pass through the mind of an interesting person. In the process something happens to it. It is no longer an inorganic substance, but it is in such form that it can easily be assimilated by other minds. It is these humanized and individualized thoughts that can be profitably held.

"Then it struck me that this is what literature means. Here we have a stock of thoughts in such a variety of forms that they can be used not only for food, but for medicine.

"During the last year, I have been working up a system of Biblio-therapeutics. I don't pay much attention to the purely literary or historical classifications. I don't care whether a book is ancient or modern, whether it is English or German, whether it is in prose or verse, whether it is a history or a collection of essays, whether it is romantic or realistic. I only ask, 'What is its therapeutic value?'"

He went on didactically, as if he were addressing a class.

"A book may be a stimulant or a sedative or an irritant or a soporific. The point is that it must do something to you, and you ought to know what it is. A book may be of the nature of a soothing syrup or it may be of the nature of a mustard plaster. The question for you to decide is whether in your condition you need to have administered soothing syrup or a mustard plaster.

"Literary critics make a great to-do about the multiplication of worthless or hurtful books. They make lists of good, bad, and indifferent. But in spite of this outcry, there is nothing so harmless as printed matter when it is left to itself. A man's thoughts never occupy so little space or waste so little of his neighbor's time as when neatly printed and pressed between the covers of a book. There they lie without power of motion. What if a book *is* dull? It can't follow you about. It can't button-hole you and say, 'One word more.' When you shut up a book, it stays shut.

"The true function of a literary critic is not to pass judgment on the book, but to diagnose the condition of the person who has read it. What was his state of mind before reading and after reading? Was he better or worse for his experience?

"If a book is dull, that is a matter between itself and its maker, but if it makes me duller than I should otherwise have been, then my family has a grievance. To pass judgment on the books on a library shelf without regard to their effects is like passing judgment on the contents of a drug store from the standpoint of mineralogy, without regard to physiology. In the glass jars are crystals which are mineralogically excellent — but are they good to eat?

"The sensible man does not jump at conclusions, but asks expert advice. But many persons, when they take up a highly recommended book, feel in conscience bound to go through to the bitter end, whether it is good for them or not.

"From my point of view, a book is a literary prescription put up for the benefit of some one who needs it. It may be simple or compounded of many ingredients. The ideas may unite in true chemical union or they may be insoluble in one another and form an emulsion.

" The essays of Emerson form an emulsion. The sentences are tiny globules of wisdom which do not actually coalesce, but remain suspended in one another. They should be shaken before using.

"Maeterlinck contains volatile elements which easily escape the careless readers. Chesterton's essays contain a great deal of solid common sense, but always in the form of an effervescent mixture. By mixing what we think with what we think we think, this effervescence invariably results.

" Dante, we are told, belonged to the Guild of the Apothecaries. It was an excellent training for a literary man. Some writers, like Dean Swift, always present truth in an acid form. Others prefer to add an edulcorant or sweetener.

" Of this Edulcorating School was Thomas Fuller, who tells how he compounded his History. 'I did not so attemper my history to the palate of the government so as to sweeten it with any falsehood, but I made it palatable, so as not to give any wilful disgust to those in present power, and procure danger to myself by using over-tart or bitter expressions better forborne than inserted — without any prejudice to the truth.'

"A book being a literary prescription, it should be carefully put up. Thus I learned, in looking up the subject, that a proper prescription contains: —

"(1) A basis or chief ingredient, intended to cure.

"(2) An adjuvant, to assist the action and make it cure more quickly.

"(3) A corrective, to prevent or lessen any undesirable effect.

"(4) A vehicle or excipient, to make it suitable for administration and pleasant to the patient.

"I do not propose to go into literary pharmacy more than to say that there are sufficient tests of what is called literary style. In regard to a book, I ask, Does it have any basis or chief ingredient? Does the Author furnish any corrective for his own exaggerations? Above all, is the remedy presented in a pleasant vehicle or excipient, so that it will go down easily?

"I have said," continued Bagster, "that certain books are stimulants. They do not so much furnish us with thoughts as set us to thinking. They awaken faculties which we had allowed to be dormant. After reading them we actually feel differently and frequently we act differently. The book is a spiritual event.

"Books that are true stimulants are not produced every year. They are not made to order, but are the products of original minds under the stress of peculiar circumstances. Each generation produces some writer who exerts a powerfully stimulating influence on his contemporaries, stirring emotion and leading to action. The book does something.

"So Carlyle stimulated his generation to work, and Ruskin stimulated it to social service and to the appreciation of Art. Tolstoy stimulated the will to self-sacrifice, and Nietzsche has overestimated the will to power. Rousseau furnished the stimulant to his generation both to a political and educational revolution. In the sixteenth century, Lord Burleigh said of John Knox, 'His voice is able in an hour to put more life in us than six hundred trumpets blaring in our ears.'

"When the stimulants are fresh, there is no difficulty in getting them into use. Indeed, the difficulty is in enforcing moderation. The book with a new emotional appeal is taken up by the intelligent young people, who form the volunteer poison squad. If the poison squad survives, the book gets into general circulation among the more elderly readers whose motto is 'Safety first.'

"It is to be noticed that the full stimulating effect of most books is lessened after they have been kept long in stock. When to-day you uncork Rousseau, nothing pops. Calvin's Institutes had a most powerfully stimulating effect upon the more radical young people of his day. It is now between three and four centuries since it has been exposed to the air, and it has lost its original effervescence.

"We must also take into effect the well-known principle of immunization. When a writer sets forth in a book certain powerful ideas, they may produce very little disturbance because everybody has had them before. There was a time when the poems of Byron were considered to be very heady. Young men went wild over them.

They stimulated them to all sorts of unusual actions. They modified their collars and their way of wearing their hair. Young men may still, as a part of their college education, read 'The Corsair,' but this required reading does not impel them toward a career of picturesque and heartbroken piracy. Pessimism has its fashions, and to-day it is realistic rather than romantic and sentimental.

"It is hard to get a blameless youth to enjoy the spiritual exultation that comes from the sense of romantic guilt, and a vast unquenchable revenge for the unfathomable injuries that came from the fact that he was born with a superior mind. But that was what our great-grandfathers felt when Byronism was in its early bloom. It was a feeling at once cosmical and egotistical. When we look at the placid, respectable portraits of our ancestors of the early nineteenth century, we can get no idea of the way in which they inwardly raged and exulted as they read, —

> " The mind that broods on guilty woes
>   Is like a scorpion girt with fire
> In circle narrowing as it glows,
> The flames around the captive close

Till inly searched with thousand throes.
    And maddening in her ire
One sole and sad relief she knows,
The sting she nourished for her foes.

" 'That means me,' says the promising young reader as he inwardly rages because he is girt in by a commonplace community that stupidly refuses to acknowledge itself as his foe — in fact, does n't know that he's there. What he wants is a foe on whom he can vent his poetic ire. When he can't find one, he falls into a mood of delicious self-pity.

" The vacant bosom's wilderness
    Might thank the pain that made it less;
    We loathe what none are left to share,
    Even bliss.

.   .   .   .

The keenest pangs the wretched find
    Are rapture to the dreary void,
    The leafless desert of the mind,
    The waste of feeling unemployed.

" There you have it. In each generation the pathetic consciousness of youth is of the waste of feeling unemployed. Byron appealed to the spiritually unemployed. But as an employment agent he was less successful. The only employment he suggested was a general vindictiveness.

The heart once thus left desolate, must fly at last from ease to hate. It almost seems that the remedy was worse than the disease. But our great-grandfathers, before they had troubles of their own, got a great deal of stimulation from Byron."

"But Byron," I said, "did more than that to his readers."

"Yes," said Bagster, "Byron was a real stimulant."

"Biblio-therapy is such a new science that it is no wonder that there are many erroneous opinions as to the actual effect which any particular book may have. There is always room for the imagination in such matters. There has been a great change in the theory of stimulants. Here is a little book published in Saco, Maine, in 1829. It is 'Stewart's Healing Art,' by the Reverend W. Stewart, D.D., of Bloomfield, Somerset, Maine. Dr. Stewart, when he turned from theology to medicine, lost none of his zeal. He was a great believer in very strong remedies. In regard to the treatment of nightmare, he says, 'It arises from a tarry condition of the blood. Half an ounce of my stimulating bitters, half an ounce of powders put in a quart of good rum will cure the patient.'

" I fear that among Dr. Stewart's parishioners nightmare was a recurrent disease.

" Physiologists have recently exploded the notion that alcohol is a stimulant. They now tell us that it is a depressant. The man who has imbibed freely feels brilliant, but he is n't. He is more dull than usual, but he does n't know it. His critical faculty has been depressed, so that he has nothing to measure himself by. He has lost control of his mental machinery, and he is not strong enough to put on the brake.

" Here is a stock of literary depressants which have been manufactured in large quantities. Here is a writer who turns out a thriller every six months. Every book has the same plot, the same characters, the same conclusion. The characters appear under different aliases. Their residences are different, but one might compile a directory of these unnoted names of fiction.

" Here is a book that conveys the impression that it is perfectly shocking. The author speaks of his work with bated breath. It is so strong. He wonders why it is allowed. And yet it contains nothing which the adult person did n't know before he was born. As for his newly discovered substitutes for ethics, they were the moral platitudes of the cave-dwellers. The habitual reader who imbibes these beverages thinks that he is exhilarated. What he needs is a true stimulant, something that will stimulate his torpid faculty.

" There are other books which are often confused with true stimulants but which are really quite different both in their composition and effects — they are the counter-irritants.

" A counter-irritant is a substance employed to produce an irritation in one part of the body in order to counteract a morbid condition in another part. Counter-irritants are superficial in their application, but sometimes remarkably efficacious. In medical practice, the commonest counter-irritants are mustard, croton-oil, turpentine, and Spanish flies. In recent Biblio-therapeutic practice the commonest counter-irritant is Bernard Shaw. There are cases in which literature that produces a state of exasperation is beneficial.

" Here is a case in my practice. — A. X.

Middle-aged. Intelligence middling. Circumstances comfortable. Opinions partially ossified but giving him no inconvenience. Early in life was in the habit of imbibing new ideas, but now finds they don't agree with him, and for some years has been a total abstainer. Happily married — at least for himself. Is fully appreciative of his own virtues and has at times a sense of moral repletion. Is averse to any attempt at social betterment that may interfere with his own comfort.

"He didn't come to me of his own accord — he was sent. He assured me that there was nothing the matter with him and that he never felt better in his life.

"'That is what I understood,' I said. 'It is that which alarmed your friends. If you will coöperate with us, we will try to make you so uncomfortable that in your effort to escape from our treatment you may exercise faculties that may make you a useful member of society.

"'You must read more novels. Not pleasant stories that make you forget yourself. They must be searching, drastic, stinging, relentless novels, without any alleviation of humor or any sympathy with human weakness designed to make you miserable. They will show you up.

"'I will give you a list with all the ingredients plainly indicated according to the provision of the pure food and drug law. Each one will make you feel bad in a new spot. When you are ashamed of all your sins, I will rub in a few caustic comments of Bernard Shaw to make you ashamed of all your virtues. By that time you will be in such a state of healthy exasperation as you have not known for years.'"

"How did it come out?" I asked.

"That time I lost my patient," said Bagster. "It is curious about irritants, so much depends on the person. To some skins glycerine is very irritating. And there are some minds that are irritated by what is called gentle irony.

"Here is one of the most irritating things ever written," he said, picking up Daniel Defoe's "Shortest Way with the Dissenters." "To read 'Robinson Crusoe' one would n't suppose that its author could drive his contemporaries almost frantic. There was nothing sharp about Defoe's style. He did not stab his opponents with a rapier-like wit. His style was always circumstantial. His manner was adhesive. Seriously and earnestly as one who was working for good, he sought out the most sensitive spot and then with a few kind words he applied his blistering adhesive plaster. No wonder Defoe had to stand on a pillory."

"I suppose," I said, "you would class all satires as counter-irritants."

"No," said Bagster. "Pure satire is not irritating. It belongs not to medicine, but to surgery. When the operation is done skillfully, there is little shock. The patient is often unaware that anything has happened, like the saint in the old martyrology who, after he had been decapitated, walked off absent-mindedly with his head under his arm."

Bagster opened the door of a case labeled Antipyretics. It contained what at first seemed an incongruous collection of books, among which I noticed: "The Meditations of Marcus Aurelius," Sir Thomas Browne's "Urn-Burial," Trollope's novels, the Revised Statutes of Illinois, the poems of Ossian, Gray's "Elegy," a history of Babylon, "Sir Charles Grandison," Young's "Night Thoughts," and Thomas

Benton's "Thirty Years in the United States Senate."

"I don't pretend that this collection has any scientific value. My method has been purely empirical. There are remedies that I have tried on individual patients. An antipyretic is something which depresses the temperature; it is useful in allaying fevers. I should not put these books in the same class except for therapeutic purposes. They have a tendency to cool us off. You know Emerson tells us how, on coming out of the heated political meetings, Nature would put her hands on his head and say, 'My little man, why so hot?' And there are books that do the same for us.

"It takes a person of a philosophic mind to respond to the antipyretic influence of Marcus Aurelius. One of my patients confessed that in attempting to reach those philosophic heights he 'felt considerable het up.'

"In cases where the conscience has been overstimulated by incessant modern demands, I find Trollope a sovereign remedy. After unsuccessful attempts to live up to my own ideals, as well as to those of my neighbors, I drop down into the Cathedral Close, Barchester, and renew my acquaintance with Bishop Proudie and his excellent lady and the Dean and Chapter, including the minor canons. Everything is so morally secure. These persons have their ideals, and they are so easily lived up to. It is comforting now and then to come into a society where every one is doing his duty as he sees it, and nobody sees any duty which it would be troublesome for him to do.

"Here is a somewhat different case. A. J. came to me complaining of great depression of spirits. On inquiry, I found he was a book-reviewer on a daily paper. I suspected that he was suffering from an occupational disease. Said that nobody loved him, he was a literary hangman, whose duty it was to hang, draw, and quarter the books that were brought to him for execution. Nobody loves a hangman. Yet he was naturally of an affectionate disposition. I found that he was a man of fastidious taste, and a split infinitive caused him acute pain. Our social worker called at the house and found that besides the agony caused by reading so many poor books, he had financial anxiety. The boss had said that if he continued to be so savage in his criticisms, he would lose his job. He has a wife and three children.

"I talked to him soothingly about the general state of literature. It was too much to expect that a faultless masterpiece should be produced every week. It is hard enough to get people to read masterpieces, as it is. If they were produced in greater quantities, it might be fatal to the reading habit.

"'You set your standard too high at the beginning. You are like a taxicab driver who sets the hands of the dial at the seventy-five cent mark before he starts his machine. This discourages the passenger. If it costs so much to stand still, he thinks it would be better to get out and walk. Start the day with some book that can be easily improved upon.'

"I gave him a copy of the 'Congressional Record.' 'Every day before you sit down to your pile of new books, read a chapter of this voluminous work.'

"Yesterday he told me he had read a hundred pages. 'By the way,' he said, 'I have noticed a marked improvement in our young writers, whose books come to my desk. Their style seems so clear and their expressions are so concise.'

"After spending a certain time every day in reading the works of our lawmakers he had learned many lessons of literary tolerance. He used to be annoyed because every one was n't as critical as he was. Now he is inclined to treat criticism as a special interest.

"He read with approval a revelation concerning the Apocrypha given in 1833 to one of the Latter-day Saints. 'Thus said the Lord unto you concerning the Apocrypha. There are many things contained in it that are true, and there are many things contained in it that are not true. Whoso readeth it let him understand it. Whoso is enlightened shall obtain benefit. Whoso is not enlightened cannot be benefited. Therefore it is not needful that the Apocrypha should be translated.'

"There is a great deal of sense in that. Those who are enlightened enough to read the Apocrypha will be benefited. Those who cannot be benefited will not read it. Perhaps it's just as well.

" I have a patient, an aspiring politician, who almost went to pieces through his excessive devotion to his own interests in the last campaign. As he had identified his interests with those of his country, when he lost the election he felt that the country was ruined. He could, he told me, have stood his personal disappointment, but the sudden collapse of public righteousness was too much for him. Marcus Aurelius, Epictetus and Sir Thomas Browne's 'Urn-Burial' had no effect in allaying his feverish symptoms. I had him recite Gray's 'Elegy' for three successive mornings. But the clinical chart showed that his temperature continued above normal.

"Quite by accident, I recalled the volumes of Senator Benton. As a child I had often looked at them with awe in my grandfather's library. They were my symbol of Eternity. Thirty years in the United States Senate seemed such a long time.

"I recommended the volumes to my patient. Yesterday he informed me that he felt differently about the election. He talked quite rationally and with a certain detachment that was encouraging. He had been thinking, he said, that perhaps thirty years after nobody would remember who gained this election. A great many things, he said, happen in this country in the course of thirty years that are not so important as they seem at the time. Indeed the antipyretic action of Benton's book was so great that I feared that he might be cooled down too much, so that as a corrective I administered a tincture of Roosevelt.

"I have a patient who had been a stockbroker and had retired, hoping to enjoy his leisure. But the breaking-up of his accustomed habits of thought was a serious matter. His one intellectual exercise had been following the market, and when there was no market for him to follow, he said he was all broken up.

"He came to me for advice and after detailing his symptoms asked if I couldn't give him a bracer; perhaps I could recommend a rattling good detective story. I notice that a large number of my patients want to furnish both the diagnosis and the treatment, expecting me only to furnish a favorable prognosis. I am told by medical friends that they have the same experience.

"I sat down with my patient and talked with him about occupational diseases. I do not hold with some that a steady occupation *is* a disease. It only makes one liable to certain maladies. It upsets the original balance of Nature. You know Shakespeare says 'Goodness growing to a pleurisy dies in his own too much.' Too-muchness in one direction leads to not-enoughness in another.

"'You have had an overdevelopment of certain virtues. You must restore the balance. For years your mind has been on the jump. It is like a kitten that will follow a mouse or a string as long as it is moving rapidly. You have been obsessed with the idea of price, and when you can't learn the price of anything you think that it has ceased to exist. It is as if you had spent all your life in a one-price clothing store where every garment had a tag indicating its exact value in dollars and cents. You are suddenly ushered into a drawing-room where you see a great many coats and trousers moving about without any tags. You go away feeling that the clothing business has gone to pieces. You need to learn that some things exist that are not for sale.

Now I propose a thorough emotional reëducation. Your mind has been interested only in rapidly moving objects to which you, at each moment, ascribe a specific value. I want to turn your mind to the vague, the misty, the imponderable. Each day you are to take exercises in nebulosity. You are to float away into a realm where being and not being, doing and not doing, knowing and not knowing amount to very much the same thing.'

"My patient rebelled. He said his wife had taken him once to a lecture on the Vedanta philosophy, and he felt that his constitution could n't stand that treatment.

"'I understand,' I said. 'Orientalism does not agree with some constitutions. I will try something that appeals to ancestral feelings.'

"I then arranged a set of daily exercises. It was based on the principle of a well-known teacher of longevity, who advises that we masticate our food diligently till it disappears through involuntary swallowing. I directed the patient to fix his mind on the price of his favorite stock, at the same time reading aloud a chapter of Ossian. He was to keep this up till the thought of the stock disappeared through involuntary inattention.

"The cure is slow, but is progressing. I began by giving the patient as a thought to hold, the price of a hundred shares of New York, New Haven and Hartford Railroad. He was to hold the thought as he paced his room, inhaling deeply and reading, —

"'A tale of the days of old, the deeds of the days of other years.

"'From the wood-skirted fields of Lego ascend the gray-bosomed mists. Wide over Lora's stream is poured the vapor dark and deep. The spirit of all the winds strides from blast to blast, in the stormy night. A sound comes from the desert. It is Conar, King of Innisfail. His ghost sat on a gray ridge of smoke.'

"'That is a queer thing for him to sit on,' said my patient.

"I was greatly encouraged by this remark. He had got his mind off the stock. The cure was working. 'Keep your eye on the ghost,' I said. 'There he is — "with bending eyes and dark winding locks of mist."'

"After half an hour of rhythmic chanting, I

found that his anxieties about the stock market had evaporated in an Ossianic mist, leaving his mind quite cool and composed. Yesterday when I made a professional call, I found him reciting the praise of Tel. & Tel.

"'Dreams descended on Larthon, he saw seven spirits of his fathers. Son of Alpin strike the string. Is there aught of joy in the harp. Pour it on the soul of Ossian. Green thorn of the hill of ghosts, that shakest thy head to nightly winds! Do you touch the shadowy harp robed with morning mists, when the rustling sun comes forth from his green-headed waves.'

"He said he did n't have the slightest idea what it all meant, but he felt better for reciting it. He saw that he had been starved for this sort of thing. There was something misty and moist about the words. He liked the feel of them. If I had n't prescribed Ossian, he might have taken to futurism. Shadowy harps, and green-headed waves and gray ghosts sitting on a ridge of smoke were just the thoughts he needed. They made the business world seem so much less uncertain.

"After that, I had a little talk about mental

hygiene. 'What you said about the moist feeling of the words is very true. In these days of artificial heating and artificial lighting, we keep our minds too dry. We ought to have a spiritual hygrometer and consult it. While our consciousness may be all right, our subconsciousness suffers from the lack of humidity in our mental atmosphere. You know that our ancestors were people of the mists.'"

Bagster expounded the theory of literary antitoxins. "Each age has," he said, "its peculiar malady. There is one point on which everybody is abnormal. There is a general obsession which affects all classes. For a time, everybody thinks and feels in a certain way—and everybody is wrong. The general obsession may be witchcraft, or religious persecution, or the eternal necessity of war, or the notion that we can get something for nothing. Whatever the notion is, everybody has it.

"Ordinary minds succumb to the epidemic. Unusually strong minds overcome the toxic elements of the time and recover. In their resistance they produce more antitoxin than they need for themselves. This can be used for the benefit of others.

"Thackeray could not have written the 'Book of Snobs,' if snobbery had not been a malady of his time which it required a special effort on his part to overcome.

"Plutarch's 'Lives' is a powerful antitoxin for the evils of imperialism. But Plutarch lived when the Roman Empire was at its height. Plutarch's men were not the men he saw around him. They stood for the stern republican virtues which were most opposed to the tendencies of his age.

"One great use of the antitoxins is in the treatment of various forms of bigotry." Bagster showed me a cabinet over which he had inscribed the prayer of Father Taylor, "O Lord save us from bigotry and bad rum. Thou knowest which is worse."

He had shelves labeled — Catholic Bigotry, Protestant Bigotry, Conservative Bigotry, Progressive Bigotry, and the like. "When I first began to treat cases of this kind I tried to introduce the patient to some excellent person of the opposing party or sect, thinking thus to counteract the unfavorable impression that had been formed. But I soon found that this treatment was based on a mistake and only aggravated the symptoms. A bigot is defined as one who is illiberally attached to an opinion, system, or organization. His trouble is not that he is attached to an opinion, but only that he is illiberally attached. My aim, therefore, is to make him liberally attached. To that end I try to make him acquainted with the actual thoughts of the best men of his own party and to show him that his inherited opinions are much more reasonable than he had supposed. After I have got my patient to recognize the best in his own party, I then introduce him to the same kind of person in another party. At least that is my plan."

"As a matter of fact," I asked, "do you have many patients who come to be cured of their intolerance?"

"No," said Bagster, "people very seldom come to a physician unless their disease causes them some pain. Now, intolerance causes no pain to the intolerant person. It is the other fellow who suffers."

"And I suppose it is the other fellow who complains?"

"Yes, generally," said Bagster. "The fact is that most persons prefer the toxins in their system to the antitoxins. Before you can do much for them, you must overcome their prejudices."

"But in this case the prejudice is the disease."

"Yes, and the getting them to see it is the treatment."

Just at this moment Bagster was called away by a patient who had taken an overdose of war literature. I was sorry, because I wished to discuss with him books which are at the same time stimulants and sedatives. They put new life into us and then set the life pulse strong but slow.

Emerson says,

> That book is good
> Which puts me in a working mood.
> Unless to thought is added will
> Apollo is an imbecile.

The book which puts us in a working mood is one which we are never able to read through. We start to read it and it puts us in a mood to do something else. We cannot sit poring over the printed page when our work seems suddenly so interesting and well worth while. So we go about our work with a new zest.

This seems very ungrateful, but when our working mood has exhausted itself, we return to our energizing volume with that kind of gratitude which has been defined as "the lively expectation of favors to come."

THE ALPHABETICAL MIND

WHEN Gulliver visited Lagado he found that the philosophers of that literary center had been grappling with the difficulties of language. Anticipating the reforms of the futurists, they had simplified their speech by leaving out all unnecessary words and confining themselves to nouns. Then it occurred to some of the more advanced thinkers that the noun was only the symbol of a thing. Why not converse by the simple and rational method of pointing directly to the thing itself?

Henceforth the vocabulary of the realistic Lagadian was identical with his worldly possessions. When making an afternoon call, he would carry with him articles which would serve for small talk. Gulliver observed that the more highly intellectual citizens found it necessary to have servants who carried their conversational conveniences in baskets. The ordinary person, however, got along very nicely with the subjects he could take with him in his pocket.

When we consider the Lagadian method of intellectual intercourse, we are struck by the fact of the extreme limitation in the subject-matter. But what is lacking in variety is made up in clearness.

Persons of a disputatious turn of mind were spared many fallacies. They could not be troubled by the *ignoratio elenchi*, or the undistributed middle, or the argument in a circle, or any of the bugbears of formal logic. When they changed the subject, every one knew that it was changed. The old subject was wrapped up and put back into the basket, and a new subject was taken out carefully and dusted and set on the table for discussion. In short, in Lagado there never was the slightest difficulty in determining what you were talking about. There it was. You might approve or disapprove, but when two persons were in the same room, they were seeing the same thing.

It is just here that our ordinary intellectual machinery breaks down. We try to communicate by means of words. We express our thoughts in a way that is perfectly clear to ourselves. We pass moral judgments based on conscientious reasoning; but we are never sure that our interlocutor is thinking about the same things. To him the words may suggest a quite different set of facts.

It is in vain that we appeal to the dictionary, that Hague Tribunal of words. Its solemn adjudications usually evade the point at issue. It tells us what a word means, and then proceeds to explain that it means something else. It may have a dozen significations each supported by good authorities.

You think you know what the word "deacon" means, for you know a deacon and esteem him highly. You turn to the dictionary and you find that in ecclesiastical usage the word "deacon" has ten different meanings, according to the church you happen to belong to or to the century you are interested in. A deacon of the Apostolic Church was an officer who took care of the poor. A Roman Catholic deacon is quite a different person from a Presbyterian deacon. If you are curious to know what a Mormon deacon is like you are referred to the Mormon Catechism,

Chapter XVII. But this is merely ecclesiastical usage. You are told that in Scotland deacon is the title of the president of an incorporated trade and chairman of its meetings. But all this does not help you to understand the next definition — "A green salted hide or skin weighing not less than seven pounds."

In Lagado they would avoid all this ambiguity. The gentleman who was wishing to talk about a salted hide weighing not less than seven pounds would bring one with him. It would be evident that this was a very different subject from that presented in the form of an officer of the church. But when we use words we cannot judge what is meant except by the context. And the context being formed of other words which are also multi-meaningful, it is often a case of the blind leading the blind.

Sometimes the mind falls between two meanings and suffers a serious shock. Take such a word as "law." We talk of natural law, the laws of health, the laws of Missouri, international law. I have heard an earnest clergyman exhort his hearers to obey a law of nature — as if they could do otherwise. He had passed from the idea of law as a rule of conduct prescribed by authority, and which we are bound to obey, to law as a proposition which expresses the constant or regular order of certain phenomena. I can break the laws of the commonwealth, and if I am found out the penalties provided for such action may be visited upon me. But if I willfully jump off a cliff I do not break the law of gravitation. I only illustrate it. The consequences, however painful to me, are not of the nature of legal penalty.

A word will often carry associations from one sphere into another. To the ordinary American the Monroe Doctrine carries with it a certain authority and sanctity. It comes from the word "doctrine," which he associates with religion rather than with politics. A doctrine is something to be believed, and publicly professed. The American is a professor of the Monroe Doctrine. It is a part of a creed that must be accepted as a test of membership. He may not understand it, but he should not be skeptical in regard to it. Suppose, instead of calling it the "Monroe Doctrine," we should call it the "Monroe Policy." Immediately his mental attitude would be altered.

He passes out of what the theologians call "dogmatics" into a region of free thought. A policy is something that can be changed to fit the times.

There are purists who have a superstitious veneration for the dictionary. To them the lexicographer is a priest who by the authority vested in him joins together the word and its meaning in indissoluble wedlock. As a matter of fact, he is only a gossip who observes the doings of words. His respect for "good usage," which so often imposes on us, is based on nothing more than "they say." They say that a certain word and a certain meaning are "keeping steady company." How long it will keep up nobody knows.

The stories of the flirtation of words collected by inquisitive philologists fill huge volumes. A literal-minded person is filled with consternation over the record of verbal inconstancy. One hardly sees how a single word could take up with so many meanings.

It is when we come to moral decision that the great difficulty of verbal indefiniteness is most keenly felt. We are all the time passing judgment on matters of conduct. We try to express that most fundamental of all judgments — the difference between right and wrong. But while the moral sense is the most distinctive thing in normal human beings, its specific judgments are most bewilderingly contradictory. We appeal to conscience as the arbitrator, and we find the dictates of conscience leading to continual strife. Using the same moral formula peoples of different training and temper come to the most opposite conclusions. And the further civilization advances and the more various our experience, the more the chances of misunderstanding increase.

When a new thought comes we do not coin a new word to express it; we take an old word, and give it a new shade of meaning, to the increasing confusion of the simple-minded. For the old meaning is not discarded; it still survives and at any moment may assert itself.

Now, when thoughts are changing and the words remain the same, the break between them may have disastrous consequences. Sometimes it seems as if the whole fabric of modern civilization were a Babel tower destined to be ruined because of the difficulty of making the workmen understand one another. The complexity and magnitude of the task is not matched by flexibility of language.

What shall we do when we become conscious of this confusion of tongues? One way is to turn our backs on modern civilization and try to return, intellectually and morally, to the simple life. In that case we shall try like the Lagadians to limit our thoughts to things which we are able to grasp.

In this insistence on simplicity we see a curious similarity between idealists like Tolstoy and the militarists and commercialists whom they abhorred. They alike felt the necessity of reversing the order of evolution. Instead of progress from the homogeneous to the heterogeneous, they would move from the heterogeneous to the homogeneous. Their world should be all of a piece. They would eliminate all that interfered with its self-consistency.

The militarist would bring his nation to the utmost state of preparedness for war. To this end he would sacrifice personal liberty, all those moral ideas which might interfere with the sole end of national organization. The man of business would make equal sacrifices for his ideal of absolute efficiency. The idealist who works for peace as often conceives it with equal simplicity. It is a beautiful state to be attained by a return to primitive conditions of life.

But there is another way of facing the modern world. Recognizing the fact that it is becoming increasingly complicated, we may accept that complexity as involved in the evolutionary process. What we need to do is to adjust ourselves to the complex realities. Our progress must be along the line of further inventions. There are difficult tasks which await us; we must invent labor-saving machinery that will enable us to do quickly and effectively that which must be done.

The sense of bewilderment which characterizes our time is explained by our lack of modern conveniences for thinking. We are without sufficient tools for our large and coöperative work.

One great invention, which has perhaps done more than any other to expedite human communication, has been only partially followed out, — the invention of the alphabet.

Men were, indeed, able to read long before they conceived the idea of an alphabet.[1] Picture-writing must have occurred to a great many minds independently. It was not very different from the Lagadian method of communication. Instead of sending a thing to one at a distance, it would be a saving in labor to send a rude picture of the object. The further development of the idea was inevitable. The pictures could be conventionalized and combined. Not only nouns and verbs, but other parts of speech could be indicated in pictograms. But though picture-writing answered very well for a simple state of society where the thoughts to be communicated were very few, it became increasingly difficult as the number of words to be written increased. For each word, or at least syllable, had to have a symbol of its own. Reading and writing became very difficult. There were so many symbols to learn and remember.

Then came the epoch-making discovery of the alphabet. It represents a triumph of analysis and synthesis. It was found that it was not necessary to make a picture at all. The sounds of the language were distinguished and reduced to a very few elements. These phonetic elements were indicated by certain letters. Once having learned the value of the letters, they could be put together in any way that might be desired. Even in our imperfect alphabet we can with twenty-six letters form all the words that are in our language. If we desire to make new words, the same letters can be used. There is no confusion. Even a child can do it. Of course a child cannot learn the alphabet as quickly as he can learn to read a few simple words without spelling. If you wish him to recognize the word "cat," it is not necessary that he should painfully spell our *c-a-t*. Write the word beside a picture of a cat and he sees the point. Likewise dog and rat and other animals may he recognized in this pictorial way without any strain on the power of analysis.

But the difficulty comes when you pass from these simplicities to more complex actualities. Suppose, instead of "cat" you write it "act." There is a family resemblance between the two written forms. The child naturally infers that "act" is a different kind of a cat.

Then you must confront him with the highly

intellectual task of spelling. The child sees each letter standing in its integrity. *A* has a sound of its own and so has *C* and so has *T*. These letters will join in spelling "cat," but they have no prejudices in favor of such a combination. They will just as readily join with other letters to form any other animal. These vowels and consonants have no preferences that prevent them from making any word that may happen to be needed. But whatever company they are in, they have a value of their own.

If we are to emerge from our moral and intellectual confusion, we must extend further the principle of the alphabet. In the decisions of the questions that most concern us, we are still in the stage of picture-writing. We are, strictly speaking, illiterates. We recognize symbols and pictures; but we do not know our letters, and we cannot put them together. Our moral education has not reached the alphabetic style of culture.

For the child the pictorial method is necessary. He is not capable of forming abstract ideas or of becoming interested in them. For him seeing is the only kind of believing. It is in vain to define goodness, but he knows a good man. His father is a good man, and in a lesser degree his uncles and cousins, the degree of goodness varying inversely as the distance of the relationship. All sorts of admirable qualities may be recognized in his family and neighborhood. These virtuous people form excellent illustrations of ethical truths. They serve to show him pictures of goodness.

Now, if he were always to remain with these people, there would be no reason why these pictures should not suffice for his moral expression. When the well-meaning person was confined to dealing with his own clan, this method did suffice.

But the modern man has been emancipated. He is compelled to meet all sorts of people. In a democracy he must, in order to deal justly, take upon himself responsibilities that once were reserved for statesmen. He must get into right relations, not with a few neighbors, but with a vast variety of persons and situations.

By those of old time we have been told of the duties we owe to our neighbors: but the question, Who is my neighbor? comes with the startling sense of novelty. We have so many new neighbors. We have pictures in our minds of admirable characters—the brave, the true, the just, the generous. *Our* soldiers are brave. Our hearts thrill as we think of their daring deeds of loyalty. But are we able to recognize the brave man who does not wear our uniform? Can we recognize a brave enemy? A martyr is a man who dies for what he conceives to be the truth. We have visions of the noble army of martyrs. But these faithful witnesses all seem to agree with us. They are the people who died for the things we believe in. But what of those whose opinions did not coincide with ours? They died for ideas which do not commend themselves to us. Do they belong to the noble army? The fact is we are able to recognize a few combinations that have been made familiar to us. But we are not able to read at sight the characters that pass before us with such bewildering rapidity. To know a good man when we see him is not easy, if he happens to come from a different neighborhood, and have strange manners, or wear outlandish clothes.

The old-fashioned spelling-match used to begin tamely with words of one or two syllables

which the least unskilled could master; then it
rapidly mounted to words never used in common
speech but which were the alpine summits of
orthography. Those who had fallen by the way
looked up admiringly at the mountaineers scal-
ing polysyllabic pinnacles. How surprising were
the adventures and misadventures. One might
mount to the summit of Sesquipedality and yet
on his return to the lower level fall into a cre-
vasse that yawned between *e* and *i*.

In a moral spelling-match it would not be
necessary to give out any but the most familiar
words, for we are all beginners and are easily
confused. Spell "Christian virtue." How many
eager hands are upraised — theological profes-
sors, preachers orthodox and liberal, devout
church members, philosophers, historians!

How many ways they spell it! There seems
to be no agreement as to the elements of which
it is composed. Wherein does Christian virtue
differ from any other kind of virtue?

Several years ago I happened to be on a committee to arrange the programme of a conven-
tion interested in practical religion. We had a
morning devoted to Christian ideals in business.

We wished to have speak to us a number of business men who had been successful in doing business in accordance with the Golden Rule. They would tell us their experience. A number of names were suggested by different members of the committee. When the names were all in, the chairman remarked, " Gentlemen, has it occurred to you that all these Christians are Jews?"

It reminded me of the embarrassment which must have come to those who asked, Who is our neighbor? and were told the story of the man who had fallen among thieves. It was a beautiful story and illustrated precisely what they had been taught to recognize as that which was most characteristic in Hebrew virtue. How irritating, when their moral sentiments were flowing in the traditional channel, to have a complexity added — he was a Samaritan. They could recognize a good Jew. It formed a familiar picture. But a good Samaritan — that was no picture at all. And they did not know how to spell.

For the good Jew to recognize the existence of the good Samaritan involved a moral reëducation. He must set free the idea of goodness from the idea of nationality with which it had been invariably connected. He must do what the printer does when he distributes the type. They have printed to-day's news. To-morrow the same letters in different combinations must print quite different words. Many persons have no facilities for distributing moral type. Early in life their minds are made up. Henceforth all their impressions are made from stereotyped plates.

Not being able to express these new choices in the stereotyped form, they cease to think of them as having any moral significance. The man was an idealist in his youth. Now he is compelled to conform to what he considers an unmoral world. Conscious of the increasing discrepancy between his practice and his principles, he becomes either a cynic or a sentimentalist. His conscience only makes him querulous. In his judgment of other people he is bitter. He has a definite picture of what they ought to be. Their lack of correspondence to that mental picture is an evidence of their hypocrisy.

The man with the alphabetical mind is able

to deal with the actual world much more steadily and effectively. His moral ideals are not in a glutinous mass, adhering to some concrete form. They are easily detachable. He recognizes a few elements which always retain the same values, but which may unite to form all sorts of compounds.

When he admires sincerity, he has recognized a distinct moral value. He speaks of a sincere friend, but in precisely the same way he acknowledges the sincerity of his enemy. The man is mistaken, but he is sincerely mistaken. There is a sincere believer and an equally sincere skeptic. The two have much more in common than they realize. The quality of sincerity manifests itself differently in a man of science and in an artist, but it is essentially the same virtue. Now, sincerity is always admirable in itself, but it is only a single letter in the moral alphabet, and it may be used in spelling many unpleasant words.

A bigot is often sincere and so is a prig. One may heartily acknowledge their good qualities and yet be sincerely desirous of avoiding their company.

Moralists have a way of treating certain virtues or vices as if they were inseparable. They tell us, for example, that a bully is always a coward while the brave are the gentle. Such combinations form pictures that are easily recognizable. But, unfortunately, it is not safe to judge human nature in this pictorial fashion. The next bully we meet may not be so easily scared as we should desire. He may be of the courageous variety.

A man may be learned and yet lacking in common sense. He may be selfish, efficient, narrow-minded, enthusiastic, devout, good-natured, healthy, and affectionate. And he may exhibit these traits singly or in any conceivable combination. He may be a genuine philanthropist addicted to sharp dealing. He may be a mystic, hard and cruel. He may be a saint with a rich vein of humor. In short, you can never tell what he is till you know him intimately.

In passing sweeping judgments we may see one characteristic and then around it we build a character to match. We have an elaborate set of inferences which are usually wrong in proportion as they are logical. It is so much easier to condemn than to understand. The conscience staggers along under a load of indiscriminating judgments. It is the lazy man's burden.

To come down from the judgment seat and take our place in the spelling-class is a sore trial to our pride. We have no longer a chance for that splendid, confident dogmatism which is so becoming to us. Our pictures of faultless heroes and utterly wicked foes lose their symmetry. We are not so sure of ourselves as we should like to be, and we come upon many facts that pain us. If we had our own way, we should not acknowledge their existence; but we are not allowed to have our own way. We must spell the hard words that are given out, or else go to the foot of the class.

Spelling is a difficult business and familiar words have a strange look when we analyze them. Sometimes when we take a word apart it seems impossible to get it together again. We have to use our minds. It's not nearly so nice as the old way of looking at pictures and being told what they mean. But the teacher says that if we keep at it and really learn to spell, then we can take up the big book for ourselves and tell what it means. Before we are able to read freely we must learn our letters.

THE GREGARIOUSNESS OF MINOR POETS

BY natural disposition and by habit of life a poet is the least gregarious of human creatures. He flourishes in what Milton describes as "a pleasing solitariness." Novelists and historians must be, in some sort, men of the world. They must frequent courts and drawing-rooms and all sorts of public gatherings in order to collect material for their work. They are traffickers in other men's ideas, and they must be good mixers.

But when the poet is "hidden in the light of thought," it is his own thought. If it is different from other men's thought, all the better. It adds to the fascinating mystery of his personality. The highest praise we can give him is the acknowledgment that he has had some gift that was all his own. "His soul was like a star and dwelt apart." It is possible for him to do his best work while dwelling apart, for his business is not to interpret other men's moods, but his own.

Clergymen are inclined, when they have opportunity, to flock together in presbyteries and conferences, associations and convocations. After preaching to their congregations on Sunday they frequent ministers' meetings on Monday, where they address one another. Theodore Parker used to lament this habit, to which he ascribed some of the faults of his brethren. Ministers, he declared, are like cabbages; they do not head well when they are planted too close together. But though clerical gregariousness may be carried to an excess, a certain amount of it is necessary to the successful carrying on of the profession. Among the higher clergy the solitary habit would be obviously impracticable. When Lord Westbury was asked what were the duties of an archdeacon he answered: "The duties of an archdeacon consist in the performance of arch-diaconal functions." Now it is evident that these arch-diaconal functions cannot be performed except in connection with an ecclesiastical body. No one, however gifted, could be an archdeacon on his own hook.

So a lawyer must be a member of the bar in order to practice his profession. The physician must be in good standing in the Medical Society. A plumber cannot act as a mere individual. He does not appear like the solitary horseman in the romances. He is a recognized duality. When we send for a plumber we expect to see two. A pleasing solitariness is not allowed in his working hours.

But a poet does not need other poets to bear him company or to complete his work. He does not need a congregation to inspire him. He comes alone to his chosen reader. It is a case where two is company and three is a crowd.

The transitory nature of his inspiration adds to this tendency to solitariness on the part of the poet. It is not easy for him to keep business hours, or make contracts for work to be finished at a given time. His productive energy is inconstant. The product of industry can be counted upon and can be delivered when promised. But the poetry which is the product of industry is worthless. All the value is that which comes from some unpredictable felicity of mood. Now and then a poetical thought comes, and under the impulse of the moment he puts it into words that are really much better than he could have contrived if he had labored for them. There is a sudden snatch of real song, a phrase or two that are unforgettable. No one seems able to do these things every day. It is a great good fortune to be able to do them sometimes. A person who is subject to such accidents we call a poet.

Sometimes the poet attempts to meet the man of affairs on his own ground, and do business according to the accepted rules. He is usually mortified by his inability to "deliver the goods." In the Book of Numbers there is an illuminating story of such an attempt to control poetic inspiration. The poet Balaam had gained a considerable reputation among the Moabitish tribes for his fine flow of maledictory verse. When Balak had become alarmed over the progress of the invading Israelites, he bethought him of Balaam and his gifts. "And Balak offered sheep and oxen and sent them to Balaam."

But when Balak waited for the outburst of

rhythmical invective which he had paid for he was disappointed. Instead of curses Balaam's words turned out to be blessings of no value whatever to his employer. Instead of living up to his contract Balaam " went not as at the other times to meet with enchantments, but he set his face toward the wilderness." It was the wild nature of the poet asserting itself.

Balaam sang his song in his own way without regard to his contract, and no wonder that Balak was indignant. "Balak's anger was kindled against Balaam and he smote his hands together and Balak said unto Balaam: I called thee to curse mine enemies and behold thou hast blessed them altogether these three times. Therefore now flee thou to thy place. I thought to promote thee unto great honor, but lo, the Lord hath kept thee back from honor."

The story of the parting of the man of affairs and the poet is one that has been repeated many times. "And Balaam rose up and went and returned to his own place; and Balak also went his way."

In his natural state the poet accepts the situation cheerfully. He sets his face toward the wilderness which he loves, and is content with the inspiration which may come. But now and then among the minor poets there comes a change of temper that is most remarkable. The minor poet forgets his individuality and becomes gregarious. He is no longer content with casual inspiration and intermittent illuminations. He must be up and doing. He must coöperate. He must find those whose spiritual impulses synchronize with his own. He must choose a name which shall designate those who belong to his school. Above all, he must educate the general public to appreciate the product of coöperative genius.

In indicating that this sudden gregarious tendency is most observable among minor poets no disparagement is intended. The term "minor poet," like that of minor prophet, refers to the quantity rather than the quality of the work done. Amos was not less a prophet than Ezekiel. His book is not so large, that is all. This in a literary man may sometimes be an added claim to our regard. Gold is gold, whether found in the mother lode or in a slender vein. Some of the best poetry is the work of minor poets who left no complete poetical works. They have not created much, but they have given some words which are priceless. Who does not know the slender little volume that comes unheralded? Is so modest that it makes little demand upon time or shelf room? And yet many a bulky volume has less worth. It is the individual offering of the minor poet in his unsophisticated days. Later on a bit of his work might slip into a place in the anthologies. That is a post-mortem honor.

But when the minor poet becomes class-conscious, he is ambitious to make his first appearance in an anthology. He will not go alone up a footpath to Parnassus, if he can climb into an omnibus with his mates. The more the merrier. When the gregarious instinct is in control we no longer are conscious of the appeal of a single person. A company of new poets appears in a body and insists on the right of collective bargaining for our admiration. We must accept the New Poetry that bears the Union label, or face, the consequences.

Now in joining the union, and merging himself with a group, however excellent, the new poet is, I think, ill-advised. There are some things which cannot be done coöperatively, and poetry is one of them. It cannot be standardized or promoted. In fact there is very little that can be done about it except enjoy it when it comes.

There is nothing more delightful than the discovery of a new poet, unless it is the recovery of an old one. We are eager to hear a fresh, unspoiled voice and to be cheered by a variation on familiar themes. That in which he distinctly differs from those who preceded him is his peculiar merit. He comes with the dew of the morning upon him.

If it should happen that at about the same time another new poet should turn up that would be a happy coincidence. There is always room in the upper story for such rare visitants. Half a dozen new poets appearing simultaneously would awaken surprise. Still it would not be miraculous. Such things have happened. But the point is that each newcomer must stand on his own feet and do his work in his own way. His welcome must be all his own. The fact that he appears at the same time with others is only an accident.

The new poet is at his best before he has been

sophisticated by too much intercourse with men of his own craft. We love to watch him going his care-free way, unmindful of the Duties of the Hour or the Idols of the Tribe. He is like the shepherd in Lycidas who, when he had sung his song,

> twitched his mantle blue
> To-morrow for fresh woods and pastures new.

It was the quick gesture of one conscious of the need neither of audience nor collaborators.

It is a sad day for the new poet when he hears the call of his kind and becomes conscious that he has a duty to perform for his fellow poets in explaining and defending their innovations. In dedicating his talents to the service of the group he is guilty of futile self-sacrifice. He loses his first sense of irresponsible freedom, and after a few years he becomes a conscientious copyist of his own early manner, and an apologist for the manner of his coevals. The murderer who revisits the scene of his crime has at least the salutary experience of remorse. But the poet who continually revisits the scene of his early success has no spiritual gain; and he is kept away from fresh woods.

The gang spirit 'has its uses, but there are spheres in which it does not make for the highest excellency. A single saint is admirable, but who would not flee from a gang of saints, eager to impose their peculiar type of piety upon the community? I read of a medieval saint who, when he was invited to a rich man's table, united courtesy and asceticism by partaking of the food set before him, but at the same time unostentatiously sprinkling the rich viands with ashes. This was admirable. But if I were a rich man I should not like to entertain a dozen saints who would bring their ash-shakers to my table. I should find their mannerism offensive.

The Hebrew prophets whose words have come down to us were thorough individualists. They were solitary in their habit and spoke their words whether men heard or whether they forbore. But there were bands who were called " the sons of the prophets." These men made a profession of prophetism and wandered about prophesying collectively. We do not, however, hear of any great utterance coming from these organizations. It is the same with the sons of the poets who form schools and coteries, and who are dependent on mutual support. The co-operative effort seems to do little for the production of the kind of poetry which the world does "not willingly let die." It, however, produces a vast amount of the other kind.

Some individual breaks away from the conventions. Immediately he has a score of followers, who, by using his formula, produce what appears to be the same results. The fashion grows by a process of accretion till it becomes an old fashion and is suddenly dropped. There was a period when poetry was conceived of as the "Paradise of Dainty Devices." Poets vied with each other in the invention of conceits. Words never ventured into print in their obvious meanings. They appeared in elaborate masquerade. Even religion hid behind a masque and claimed attention by pretending to be something else. This make-believe was considered the very essence of poetry. It was the criterion by which it could be distinguished from prose.

But these "Dainty Devices" would not have pleased the poet who a century ago from the American backwoods voiced his aspirations.

O for a thousand mouths, a thousand tongues,
A throat of brass and adamantine lungs!

To the members of the school of the brazen-throated and adamantine-lunged all refinements were contemptible. They were all for strength.

Sometimes the bond of union between minor poets is educational. They feel that it is their duty to improve the mind, and they proceed to do it. I take up a volume entitled " Fugitive Poems connected with Natural History and the Physical Sciences." It is not necessary that this anthology should be dated. It obviously belongs to the middle of the nineteenth century. How pathetically these poetical fugitives flock together, seeking safety in numbers! Driven out of their habitations by the advancing hordes of Science, they attempt to obtain mercy by chanting the praise of their conquerors. We are reminded of the exiles by the rivers of Babylon from whom those who carried them away captive required a song. The poetic captives of science did their best to satisfy the demand, but soon gave up the effort and hung their harps on the willows.

It is another world which we enter when we

take up "The Nightingale or Polite Amatory Songster — A Selection of Delicate, Pathetic and Elegant Songs designed chiefly for Ladies." It was published in Boston in 1808. The principle of selection was stated: "This volume is presented to the public with no exclusive claims of patronage except those arising from the solicitude of the compiler to avoid every expression that might offend the delicacy of female modesty."

The "Amatory Songster" was but one of a vast number of volumes which belonged to what we may call the "Literature of Moral Solicitude." It seems to have occurred simultaneously to a multitude of prose writers and poets, that, in taking their pen in hand, they should avoid every expression that might give offense. That any other virtue or grace beside that of avoidance was necessary did not occur to them. Even writers who were capable of more positive and varied contributions to literature sought to answer the demand.

Oliver Goldsmith, in his collection of "Poems for Young Ladies," went even beyond the "Amatory Songster" in his solicitude. He says:

"Dr. Fordyce's excellent sermons for Young Women in some measure gave rise to the following compilation. Care has been taken to select not only such poems as innocence may read aloud without a blush, but such as will strengthen that innocence."

Goldsmith was evidently ambitious. His collection should not merely represent the current ideal of innocence. It should be the latest word in Super-Innocence. He remarks: "Poetry is an art no young lady can or ought to be wholly ignorant of. The pleasure which it gives, and indeed the necessity of knowing enough to mix in modern conversation will evince the usefulness of my design."

Now the cat is out of the bag. Poetry as a pleasure was one thing. But the more important thing was the assumed "necessity of knowing enough to mix in modern conversation." Here the gregarious motive comes in. Poetry for its own sake might be produced and enjoyed in blameless solitude. But the connection between poetry and conversation renders it necessary to put the emphasis upon timeliness. Poetry must approximate to journalism. It must have a distinct news value, and be kept up to date. No-body wants to talk about last year's fashions.

It is obvious that as the fashions in modern conversation change there will be a demand for a corresponding change in the poetry that is to be talked about. Innocence having been talked out, conversation turns to a solemn knowing-ness. We see in our own time among those who would be in the swim an insistence that poets should choose themes that satisfy the serious-minded inquirer. The more unpleasant the sub-ject is, the more meritorious. Indeed in some circles it is assumed that the poet who would ad-vance the cause of modernity must begin his campaign with a policy of deliberate frightful-ness. Having shown his ability to hack his way through the sensibilities of his readers he may afterwards yield to his native geniality.

All this is a matter of fashion. If fashion re-quired that a sound moral be tacked on to every bit of poetry, the demand would be met by those who were in close touch with the market. To do otherwise would be to invite disaster.

An eighteenth-century critic complains that the "Scribleriad" by the much-admired poet

Richard Owen Cambridge was not as popular as its merits would indicate. "The composition of the 'Scribleriad' is regular, spirited and poetic. There are few descriptions so happily imagined as the approach of an army of rebuses and acrostics." Rebuses and acrostics were in fashion; why, then, was the public so cold in its attitude towards the "Scribleriad"? The critic explains: "It is to be regretted that the author determined to avoid moral reflections, which he could easily have furnished."

Mr. Cambridge was not really up to date. If, instead of merely describing his army of rebuses and acrostics, he had explained that they symbolized the eternal warfare of virtue and vice, all would have been well, and he would have had an honorable place among the new poets.

But Mr. Cambridge may have been infected by another fashion that was just passing that was not moral at all. Another critic of about the same period alludes to "the usual anacreontics the spirit of composing which was raging a few years since among all the sweet singers of Great Britain."

I like that phrase, "the spirit of composing

which." It can be applied to so many cases in
literary history. The spirit of composing anacreontics was not the only one which raged in those
days among the more gregarious poets. There
was the great Thomas Warton who had a school
of fashionable poetry, which he defended against
all comers, for Warton was not only a poet, but
a most redoubtable critic. "As a contributor to
the literature of his country few men stood higher
than Warton." He could write pieces like the
"Triumph of Isis" and "The Pleasures of Mel-
ancholy"; but above all he believed in writing
odes. He composed odes on all subjects from the
"Ode to Spring" to an "Ode to a Grizzle Wig."
His brother Joseph was also a most highly ap-
proved clergyman, critic, and poet. This gave
an opportunity for team play.

But after a while the demand for Wartonian
poetry fell off. The biographer sadly remarks,
"The school of Warton, as it is called, has not
of late been mentioned with the respect it de-
serves." It is the fate of schools.

I came across an old volume of "The Sentimental Magazine" for 1773-74. The prospectus
was most appealing. The editor opened his heart

to his subscribers. Sentimentalism he said was in the air. The new writers were full of it. But it had not been organized. People were sentimental in spots and because they were surprised by emotion. But now the time had come for sentiment to have an organ of its own. The magazine would express the aspirations and achievements of the Sentimental School. Here, free from the annoyances of alien habits of thought, they could indulge to their hearts' content in pure feeling. The editor promised that "every number of this magazine will force the tears of sensibility from the eyes of the reader."

What became of this literary force-pump I do not know. I fancy, however, that after a time it ceased to work. We are all ready to yield to emotion when it is spontaneous, but we harden our hearts when we suspect that certain persons have entered into a conspiracy to exploit our tender feelings.

I once had a lesson which I took to heart. I had two friends, both of whom happened to be blind. It unluckily occurred to me that it would be a pleasure to them to be made acquainted.

But when I suggested this to one of them he drew himself up with dignity and said: "I decline to make acquaintances on the basis of my infirmity."

I think of this when I see the attempts to bring together poets on the ground of what seem to the prosaic mind common interests and conditions. It is assumed that those who belong to the same party or live in the same place enjoy being put in the same category. Here is a volume entitled "The Poets of Maine; a collection of specimen poems of a hundred versemakers of the Pine Tree State." The Poets of Iowa are as numerous, and the Poets of Michigan are as the leaves of the forest. Why is it that local loyalty and state pride seem to fail to furnish any real bond of union to these versemakers? I do not think of Longfellow as a Poet of Maine. He has other claims upon my regard.

A topographical term, like the "Lake Poets," may be useful for conversation or lecturing, but it serves no other end. Because a certain number of gifted persons frequented the same lovely region, it does not follow that they had a great deal in common. The absurdity of classifications according to residence is seen when we remember that Keats was characterized by spiteful contemporaries as belonging to the Cockney School. Any one less of a cockney it would be hard to find. Keats walked the London streets, but his true citizenship was in the islands

> Which bards in fealty to Apollo hold.

There have been times not far remote when it was thought a laudable undertaking to bring together collections of verse under the title "Female Poetry." Why should the female poets be segregated? A careful scrutiny of their works reveals nothing which they might not have expressed with the utmost propriety in the presence of their gentleman friends. When I think of Sappho I think of her simply as a poet. That is the way I suppose that Sappho would like to be thought of.

Nor is the technique of their art a bond of union between true poets. Such a poet may find his most natural means of expression in the familiar forms of prosody. Or he may say with Chaucer's pilgrim —

> I can nat geste — rum, ram, ruf — by lettre,
> Ne, God wot, rym hold I but litel bettre.

He may be the freest of free versifiers, but if he has the poet's gift he may take what liberties he will. It is a case when the end justifies the means. But let him not think to make us receive all who abjure rhyme and familiar metres as belonging to his class. Because we admit the actuality of a horseless carriage, it does not follow that any carriage can be made to go by the simple device of shooting the horse. Nor should the new poets pride themselves on their newness in point of time. It will soon wear off. The bond that unites a poet to his contemporaries is very slight compared to that which unites him to kindred spirits in many generations. Poetry is the timeless art.

The greater poets have always proudly declared their independence of the passing hour. The mere chronological sequences have to them little significance. Shakespeare utters his defiance.

> No, Time, thou shalt not say that I do change.
> Thy pyramids built up with newer might
> To me are nothing novel, nothing strange,
> They are but dressings of a former sight.
>
> .   .   .   .
>
> Thy registers and thee I both defy
> Not wondering at the present nor the past.

Nor is this impression of timelessness characteristic only of the supreme poets. The minor poets when they are at their best have the same gift. They snatch from our working day some blessed moments of real insight. We see something that does not belong to the passing hour. It was true a thousand years ago and it is true still. These Robin Hoods rob time for the benefit of eternity. We cannot discipline them or organize them. But we are glad that there are these merry men.

THE TAMING OF LEVIATHAN

THE frontispiece of Hobbes's " Leviathan " contains a symbolic picture that becomes terrifying only when we ponder its meaning. There is a huge figure of a man holding in his hands the scepter and crozier, symbols of political and ecclesiastical power. The figure represents one born to rule.

Or was he born? Closer inspection reveals the fact, boldly proclaimed in the text, that this ruler was not born but made. He is declared to be the "artificial man." He is made out of a vast number of little men, put together after the fashion of a picture puzzle.

But why call this artificial man, not by a human name, but after a mysterious monster of the deep? Quotations from the Book of Job make clear the reason. Leviathan represents sheer force, without pity and without respect for the individual conscience. Leviathan is less than man in that he does not love; but he is stronger than any man. He is at once subhuman and superhuman. He represents a kind of strength which terrifies because it cannot be moved by the spectacle of our helplessness. It listens to no appeal.

> Canst thou draw out Leviathan with a fish hook ?
> Or press down his tongue with a cord ?
> Canst thou put a rope into his nose ?
> Or pierce his jaw through with a hook ?
> Will he make many supplications unto thee ?
> Or will he speak soft words unto thee ?
> Will he make a covenant with thee,
> That thou shouldest take him for a servant forever ?

Leviathan knows nothing of rights or duties:—

> In his neck abideth strength,
> And terror danceth before him.
> The flakes of his flesh are joined together:
> They are firm upon him; they cannot be moved.
> His heart is as firm as a stone;
> Yea, firm as the nether millstone.
> When he raiseth himself up, the mighty are afraid.

So the Hebrew poet told of the pitiless strength of Leviathan, against whom it was useless to contend. All this, said Thomas Hobbes, is true of that "artificial man" whom we have made, and who, when once made, is our master. He is the work of our hands, but we must worship him because, if we do not, he has power to kill us, and he *will* kill us because he has no pity. He is made by us, not because we will to create him, but because we must. He like ourselves is a creature of necessity.

This artificial man is the Commonwealth or the Nation. In one sense Leviathan is an aggregation of human beings, but once formed he has interests apart from them. They must sacrifice themselves to him, and must yield implicitly to his will.

Is that will a righteous will? In one sense, yes. The artificial man can do no wrong, for he himself determines the morality of those who must obey his will. He makes the law; he enforces it. That is right which makes him strong and increases the bounds of his dominion. The individual conscience must keep silent in the presence of its master. Private scruples must give way to public expediency, which is the essence of public right. But what if the individual still protests? Leviathan will strike him dead. Surely, "upon earth there is not his like."

But if we made Leviathan, why can we not

unmake him? Living as he did amid the uncertainties of a troubled time Hobbes could not deny the fact of revolution. And when revolution became a fact, he was consistent with his theory in accepting it. Yes, you can unmake Leviathan, but only as you make another Leviathan, who is stronger than he. You stand in the same relation to this new Leviathan that you stood to the old. You have made something that is mightier than yourself. Struggle as you will, you do not escape the rule of brute force. But why does not our discontent take a more radical form? Why do we not at last in desperation refuse to create the artificial man who tyrannizes over us? Is there not such a thing as liberty? Why not let the institutions, political and ecclesiastical, decay, while each man lives his own life and obeys his own conscience? Let kings and priests perish, while the individual man obeys the inner light.

Because, says Hobbes, we are all afraid. More than anything else we fear one another. In the state of nature every man's hand is against his neighbor. A man left to himself is helpless. He must find protection somewhere. Only through organization can he find security for life and property. But where the organization gets strong enough to protect him, it becomes too strong to be directed by him. It matters not what form the organization takes, whether we call it a "kingdom" or "commonwealth," whether at the head is King Charles or Oliver, the Protector, the only thing that is left for us is obedience. Our protector must determine what for us is duty.

Hobbes presented the question of might and right as it appeared to the mind of the seventeenth century. His contemporaries were still discussing the question of the divine right of kings to rule, as it presented itself to the ecclesiastical conscience. Hobbes was sternly secular. Royalty was not to him a divine institution. His argument would work equally well with a republic. He was dealing with human necessity and natural law. The power that we must obey is of our own invention. But it has got away from us, and turns upon us, and exercises compulsion over us. We are destined to make institutions which it is impossible for us to control. There is nothing left for us but blind obedience to a force which we are powerless to resist.

Had Hobbes lived in the twentieth century his Leviathan would have been a much more formidable monster. For the natural man has not greatly increased in moral or intellectual stature, but the artificial man has grown prodigiously. Human ingenuity has increased the power of political organization without having contrived means by which it may be spiritualized. Mechanism has been perfected, while the power to direct it to useful ends has not increased.

We have awakened to a great fear. We had rejoiced because human intelligence had gained such wonderful control over the blind forces of nature. But what if it should turn out that human intelligence is itself a blind force, incapable of real self-direction? What if it is destined to create institutions which destroy its own happiness? It organizes forces which are in the end destructive. It creates an artificial man and then sacrifices to it all that makes the individual life tolerable Hobbes called his artificial man "a mortal god." What if the mortal god is satisfied with nothing but human sacrifice?

It is just at this point that we must make our stand. Leviathan is strong; that we must acknowledge, and he is likely to become stronger. We should not refuse to use his strength. But we do refuse to bow down and worship him as a god.

The fact is that civilized man has not developed so far as to be free from the animistic superstitions of his remote ancestors, who worshiped the work of their own hands. The age-long battle against idolatry must still be waged. Back of some of the most dangerous doctrines of our modern times there are ideas that are survivals of the thinking of the most primitive worshipers.

Listen to the ancient iconoclast as he taunted the idolaters: "The smith maketh an axe, and worketh in the coals, and fashioneth it with hammers, and worketh it with his strong arm; yea, he is hungry, and his strength faileth; he drinketh no water, and is faint. The carpenter stretcheth out a line; he marketh it out with a pencil; he shapeth it with planes, and he marketh it out with the compasses, and he shapeth it after the figure of a man. . . .

He falleth down unto it and worshippeth, and prayeth unto it, and saith, Deliver me; for thou art my God."

Then the prophet goes on with bitter sincerity: "None calleth to mind, neither is there knowledge nor understanding to say, I have burned part of it in the fire; yea, also I have baked bread upon the coals thereof; I have roasted flesh and eaten it: and shall I make the residue thereof an abomination? shall I fall down to the stock of a tree?"

One would have supposed that the carpenter, who with his axe and pencil and compasses had wit enough to make a wooden image that looked like a man, would also have wit enough to know that this image was not a god. He had no illusions with regard to the rest of the tree. Wood was wood when he needed fuel to bake his bread. But this piece of wood which he had hewn into human shape was to him divinity.

But suppose, instead of a superstitious carpenter, that we are addressing a company of citizens, who have fallen into an idolatrous attitude to the State. Might they not properly be addressed in much the same fashion.

You have fashioned for yourselves a god. You have made it, not out of stone or wood, but out of your own thoughts, habits, necessities. Each one of you has a measure of strength. Part of it you use for the preservation of your own lives and for the welfare of your own families. The residue goes to the building up of those common interests which belong to the State. And this is well. The Nation has no power except that which you the citizens supply. You make it what it is. It has no life apart from you. It is a great and powerful instrument which you have created and which you are to use for ends which you approve. To say that a nation is prosperous, when prosperity is not diffused among its people, is to indulge in superstition. National honor is a vain thing unless it corresponds to the ethical standard of the people who are asked to give their lives in its defense. It is really *their* honor that is involved.

Over against the animistic idea of the Commonwealth as an artificial man who has been endowed with superhuman and supermoral powers, there is slowly growing up an idea that is severely realistic. The political institution has nothing miraculous about it. It is a tool of our own making. We invented it; we use it for our own purpose. We use it, and when it ceases to serve our highest purposes, it is time to invent something better. The Nation is a huge aggregate of the interests, customs, laws, traditions, and ideals which we have in common. The loyalty of the individual citizen ceases to be a blind instinct. It is based on substantial agreement in fundamental ideas. To those who hold this conception of the State, political morality differs from personal morality only in the fact that it is more difficult, and that its operations are on a larger scale.

We are watching, in Europe, not merely a conflict between nations, but a conflict between two conceptions of the meaning of nationality. No form of fanaticism has been preached more zealously nor been carried out more ruthlessly than the worship of the State as a mortal god. The hour of disillusion is coming. This is the meaning of the growing movement for democratic control.

Here in America the Leviathan of Hobbes,

bearing the scepter and crozier, has been partially tamed. We no longer worship the symbols of political or ecclesiastical power. Our attitude toward the dignitaries of Church and State lacks servility, and often, we must confess, is lacking even in the respect that is seemly.

Nevertheless, we are not free from the worship of Leviathan as a mortal god. His power is not so much political or ecclesiastical as economic and industrial and professional. We have been organizing forces that overawe us.

The corporation is an invention, by which the individual may join his fortune with others in accomplishing work which is far beyond his own means. He finds protection here and coöperation. But as the institution grows, it makes an appeal to the imagination on its own behalf, and altogether apart from the objects for which it was originally intended.

A railroad performs the function of a common carrier. Now, when a common carrier had only a horse and cart, it was very easy to determine his relation to the public. His work was useful, but strictly limited. He was to carry goods and passengers as economically as possible along the public highway between two towns. It was well understood that it was not his business to determine where the highway should run, nor to interfere with the government of the towns.

But when competing railroads become a " system," and there is a huge army of employees, and great offices become like a capital city, and territory is annexed, and there are highly trained officials, the railroad becomes personified. It is an object of a devotion that easily becomes superstition.

We have seen railroad presidents and directors whose actions can be explained only as a kind of idolatry. They were bowing down and sacrificing to the work of their own hands. Ordinary business motives would not account for the fact that they would pay more than it was worth for property whose only use was to glorify the system. After one of these unremunerative additions to the mileage of the railroad, one hears the same kind of shout that went up from the ancient worshipers, when for the space of two hours they cried, " Great is Diana of the Ephesians."

In the mean time the stockholders whose money was invested, and the public whose goods are to be carried, are little considered. They must be prepared to sacrifice to the great Leviathan.

The thoughtful working man finds himself in a similar plight. He is confronted by a power which he himself has created, and which protects him from his enemies, but at the same time coerces him. Only through organization can he hold his own against those who would reduce his wages and lower his standard of living. But the organization becoming his master is pitiless when he tries to live his own life in freedom. When he worships it as a mortal god, it crushes him.

Nor does any one of us altogether escape the dilemma. Whoever discovers that in union there is strength is confronted by the question whether that strength is to be used or to be worshiped. He must become either an artist or an idolater.

The artist uses whatever material and whatever forces he finds at hand, but he does not allow himself to be mastered by them. And when he has finished his work, he does not fall down before it. He looks at it critically, he sees its limitations, and he plans a new work which he hopes may surpass it.

He does not worship the work of his own hands because he worships an ideal that is always beyond him. The cure for idolatry is idealism.

THE STRATEGY OF PEACE

SEVERAL years ago in the "Atlantic Monthly" I drew attention to an experiment which was being tried in a Theological Seminary in which I was interested. Money had been left by an eccentric individual to found a chair of Military Science in the Seminary. The trustees had no precedent to warrant them in rejecting any considerable gift, and therefore sought to adapt the professorship as far as possible to the peaceful ends for which the institution was founded. They were fortunate in finding a retired army officer who entered heartily into the work to which he was called. The Colonel believed that the peace-maker could never succeed until he put as much courage and skill into his work as was necessary to the successful conduct of war.

Not long ago I revisited the Seminary and spent an hour in the Colonel's classroom. I found that the events of the last two years had left their impress on him and he was less inclined to dwell on the technicalities of his art, but his interest in the subject had not abated. The subject of his lecture was — "Some Lessons of the Present War bearing on the Strategy of Peace."

He said in the popular mind there is a confusion between strategy and stratagems. A stratagem is an artifice for deceiving and surprising the enemy. In former wars there was much room for such carefully planned surprises. It was possible for a general with an inferior force, by rapid concentration at an unexpected point, to gain a decisive victory. Even so late as our Civil War, Stonewall Jackson with a mobile force was able to paralyze the operations of a much larger army. In the Shenandoah Valley, screened by mountain ramparts, he could keep the Union generals guessing.

But in the present war there have been few surprises. There have been battles which in the number of troops engaged and in casualties have outranked the famous battles of history, but they have decided nothing. Even the non-military public did not follow them with breathless interest, because there was the perception of the fact that this war is not to be decided by any single battle.

The only possibility of a decisive surprise was at the beginning. When it became evident that the German armies could not reach Paris by a sudden rush, the war settled down to a grim trial of absolute strength. There was no room for stratagems in which the weaker party might win by a clever trick.

The use of the aeroplane made surprise movements difficult, but the main consideration was the magnitude of the operations and the vast number of reserves. What does it matter if on a battle front of hundreds of miles an army is confronted suddenly by a superior force at a particular point? Men and guns can be hurried in unlimited quantities to the threatened point and the balance of force redressed. Until the reserves are actually exhausted, the fight will go on.

Strategy in the sense of stratagems has had an insignificant place in this war, but strategy in its true sense, as the art of conducting complicated military movements, has never been more wonderfully displayed. In former wars mobilization has been incomplete. Only part of the power of the nation has been brought into action. In this desperate conflict it was early seen that every bit of strength was needed. The war was a war of attrition. The aim was to collect the largest reserves possible of men and munitions and money. All possible powers must be coördinated; the plans must be made upon long lines. Only when the work of preparation had been completed could there be a decision. It is a grim, terrible business, but once begun it must go on till one party is utterly exhausted.

It is this character of the war, its stern simplicity of outline, and its tremendous scope, which distinguishes it from all former conflicts. The general fitted for the task needs not quickness or cleverness, but a broad, massive understanding, an indomitable will, and a godlike patience. He must expect no spectacular victories. The force he wields moves like a glacier and not like an avalanche.

Those who have been appalled by the dreadful character of this contest like to speak of a war against war. But I fear that they are not fully conscious of the lesson that is being taught us. They often fail to recognize the magnitude of the operations in which they are engaged. Many are still inclined to put their trust in pious stratagems by which the hosts of darkness may be outwitted. They are not fully aware of the need of thorough preparation and of world-wide coöperation. They imagine that the war against war may be won by a trick or by a sudden frontal attack.

My colleague in the chair of Homiletics tells me that there is no military maneuver which is more used by the sermonizers of the Seminary than that of Gideon. Gideon, with a force of twenty-two thousand troops, had encamped by the well of Harod. He detached all but a picked body of three hundred veterans. With these he faced the allied army of Midianites and Amalekites who occupied the north end of the valley. Their force must have been considerable, for it is said they "lay along in the valley like locusts for multitude; and their camels were without number, as the sand which is upon the seashore for multitude."

Gideon made a night attack, his three hundred men being armed only with torches, trumpets, and empty pitchers. In the panic that ensued the allied army was routed. My colleague tells me that after reading the discourses handed in for criticism, he is led to believe that the students in the Seminary put too much reliance upon the efficacy of empty pitchers.

The stratagem of Gideon was admirable for its day, but it cannot be safely repeated under modern conditions. A general will hardly be justified in sending away the majority of his troops and trusting to a small body of choice spirits. The risk is too great.

In looking over the *ante-bellum* peace literature I have been struck by the curious lack of imagination. There seemed to be no power of visualizing the field and estimating the resources of the enemy. In this the peace-makers compare unfavorably with the war-makers. You have learned from your textbook that a prudent king before he makes war sits down and "takes counsel whether he is able with ten thousand to meet him that cometh against him with twenty thousand." Such a preliminary calculation seems to have been omitted in many of the plans in the war against war. In almost every case decisive operations were proposed, while an altogether inadequate force was provided. Reliance was put upon a general panic upon the part of the enemy as the result of a sudden attack.

You remember how confident many people were, only three or four years ago, that the bankers, if they were so disposed, could stop any war that threatened seriously to interfere with business. We might safely dismiss all other agencies for keeping the peace and put our trust in this Gideon band. All they had to do would be to break their financial pitchers. Panic would do the rest. It would not take three hundred to do the trick. If a dozen of the invisible rulers of Europe would say the word they could insure peace. To stop credit would be to stop war.

There were other strategists who were equally certain that Organized Labor was strong enough to stop war between nations. Had it not already been organized into a formidable international army for this very end? Were not all workers comrades? Did they not say so? Could any war be carried on against their will? All that was needed was the threat of a general ·strike Instantly the war-makers would see the impossibility of continuing their operations.

I went into a church and heard a most sincere minister discourse on the one way to secure a lasting peace. He dismissed all the auxiliaries of the secular world-economics — diplomacy and all appeal to physical force. There should be no entangling alliances. The war against war must be waged only with spiritual weapons, and by those who were willing to trust to no arm of flesh.

The Church could stop war if it would. All that is needed is to induce people to be good. A good man will not fight. That is the long and short of it. He enlarged on this aspect of his subject through the most of his discourse so that he left little time for the consideration of the question which most interested me, What would the bad men do under those circumstances? He dismissed the question, however, with the dogmatic assertion that the bad men would n't be so bad as to keep on fighting if the good men would n't irritate them by forcible resistance.

But the minister's point of view seemed statesmanlike compared with the simple-mindedness of the militarist. He was quite sure that there was only one way to keep the peace and that was for every one feverishly to prepare for war. No nation need arm except for defense. But to be adequately defended, a nation must have the biggest army and the biggest navy in the world. Obviously only one nation can be in that position at any one time. But when all nations are striving for that ideal of perfection, it will create a dangerous situation; in fact, it will be so terribly dangerous that everybody will be afraid of everybody. There will be such an accumulation of explosives that nobody will dare light a match. In that universal fear it was supposed that there would be the power to keep the peace.

Then the great explosion came, and what men feared, happened. We were all stunned and we arose, chastened, to begin to clear away the ruins and to build anew. It is useless to twit one another about the failure of self-confident prophecies. We are all in the same boat — pacifists, militarists, socialists, business men, diplomatists. Our plans on which we prided ourselves have failed. Not one of us has been able to avert the catastrophe.

But this does not mean that we are to give up in despair. It only means that we are engaged in an undertaking so vast that we cannot expect to win by any isolated action. There must be coördination of all the forces which make for peace. We cannot afford to say to any one of them, "I have no need of thee."

Let me emphasize the word "forces." The founder of this professorship had in mind questions of dynamics. He believed in force and he thought that you should be trained into its effective application. The forces which he had especially in mind were moral and spiritual, but he took for granted that the intellectual problems were similar to those that arise whenever we use any form of energy.

In using force a fundamental consideration is that we should have enough of it. An inadequate force accomplishes nothing. It must always be measured by the resistance. Only when this resistance is actually overcome by an excess of energy is there victory. This is a point which many pacifists overlook. They praise moral force and declare that it should be sufficient in all emergencies. But the amount they produce is only sufficient for a parlor exhibition. It is enough to satisfy a company of well-disposed ladies and gentlemen who have no particular grievances. But there is not a large enough quantity to quell a hungry mob, still less to coerce a military nation intent on conquest.

It is as if one were to describe the tremendous effects of an explosion of nitro-glycerine, and then exhibit a small bottle of pure glycerine. The rocks would not be rent by this emollient. Only in the proper combination with more powerful elements, and in sufficient quantities, could one expect any notable results.

After hostilities on a large scale have once begun, to cry, "Stop the War," is like the cry of frightened passengers in a collision, "Stop the train." Everybody would like to stop the train, but nobody can do it. The trains have a horrible way of stopping themselves.

The present war will go on till its momentum is exhausted, and it will give way to that equilibrium which we, for want of a better term, call peace. But that peace which statesmen will patch up when soldiers are exhausted is not the peace for which you young gentlemen are striving. It is the peace which is made by the temporary damming of the stream, it is not the "peace that floweth as a river." It is not the peace of action, but the peace of exhaustion.

History is full of high-sounding names like the Peace of Utrecht, the Peace of Paris, the Peace of Tilsit, and the rest. They only indicate a temporary preponderance of force. They register the results of war. How little they amount to is evident to any one who will spend an hour reading a Chronology.

I open, for example, at the year 1716. "Alliance between Great Britain and the Emperor May 25." That is a good beginning. "Turks defeated by Eugène at Peterwarden Aug. 5." The Turks were always disturbers of the peace and must be put down before anything permanent can be established. "The Perpetual Peace proclaimed at Warsaw Nov. 3." There you have it, the deed is done! In the same month England establishes a Sinking Fund for the extinction of the National Debt. The economic argument against war is beginning to have its effect.

But what happens in the next ten years after Perpetual Peace was formally proclaimed at Warsaw? The chronologist goes on his monotonous way as if he were announcing the departure of trains from the Union Station. Battle of Belgrade; Sardinia invaded by the Spaniards; Siege of Fredrikhall by Charles of Sweden; France declares war against Spain; Jacobite plots in England; Buda burnt; War between Turkey and Persia." After which the powers come together to consider the preliminaries for a general peace. By that time Czar Peter had died and people had forgotten that perpetual peace had already been established at Warsaw.

It will be observed that it is taken for granted that war settles things. Peace is the interval between these outbursts of activity.

What we dream of is a state in which this will be reversed, when great and necessary changes and adjustments can be brought about peacefully. Isaiah stated the ideal: "I will make thy officers peace, and thine exactors righteousness." It is this exacting nature of a righteous peace that presents the real difficulty, and it is this difficulty you must face.

Wars arise out of a conflict of wills. One group of men earnestly desire a certain good. Their wills are thwarted by another group who stand in direct opposition. How shall they get what they desire? The quietist has an answer that is exceedingly simple. The good man can always have peace by refusing to resist. Let him cultivate meekness of spirit. By ceasing to insist on his own will he avoids conflict.

If all men cultivated this spirit it would be effective in keeping the peace, though it is doubtful if it would insure progress. The little communities founded on the abnegation of personal ambition have found it hard to hold on to their more energetic young people.

Unfortunately, the appeal of the quietist is more effective with the naturally virtuous than with the strong, self-confident sinner. So the way of the transgressor is often made easier than it should be.

It is a strategical mistake for the champion of peace to spend much time upon the naturally yielding or timid, or even upon those with whom prudential considerations prevail. These do not make wars nor are they able to prevent them.

The effort must be made to convince the strong-willed and ambitious. Whether the strong man be a hero or a ruffian, whether his purpose be righteous or unrighteous, he must be made to see one thing, and that is that there is a power that is stronger than he is. If his ends be just and righteous, he must be assured that there is a power strong enough to do for him more than he can do for himself. He must appeal to that power and trust it. If he be impelled only by selfish and brutal instincts, he must be made to see that this power will inevitably stand in his way and overwhelm him. It says to him, "Thus far shalt thou go, no farther."

War is a trial of strength. It is a glorious hazard. Peace comes when one confronts a power so assured that a trial is not needed. The result of conflict is certain.

Let us consider first the case of the hero, the strong man who, in defense of what he believes to be essential justice, takes up arms. You see the man coming out of Edom, "traveling in the greatness of his strength." Why are his garments red? He answers, "I have trodden the winepress alone, and of the people there was none with me. I trod them in mine anger and I trampled them in my fury and their life-blood was upon their garments."

These are terrible words, but before you condemn him for a bloodthirsty savage, you must remember that you have been taught to "judge not after appearance, but to judge righteous judgment." You must not judge him by his words nor by his blood-stained garments.

He comes out of Edom, and you should try to find out what has been going on in Edom which has roused him to this fury. He has been the spectator there of deeds of unspeakable cruelty. He has seen the weak tortured by triumphant and pitiless foes. He has been himself the victim of arbitrary power. "I looked and there was none to help and I wondered that there was none to uphold. Therefore mine arm brought salvation and my fury it upheld me."

The "therefore" represents the logic of the strong man in the presence of a great wrong. It is not cool logic, but logic that is aflame with passion. The premise of the argument is, "there was none to help." If that be true the conclusion is irresistible, the strong man must himself take the responsibility of righting the wrong, and he must do it with such means as he has at hand. The justification of his fury is that it upholds him in the work which he is compelled to do.

In such an emergency the real peace-maker puts his main effort, not on the effect, but on the cause. He seeks to remove the cause. "Look again," he says, "and you will see that it is not true that there are none to help. I am here to help, and behind me are mighty powers, able to do quietly and effectively what you are seeking to do violently. These powers have been organized for this very purpose, and their working is sure."

If the hero can be convinced that there is an adequate power to do justice by orderly processes he lays down his arms. But before he disarms he makes sure that there is something more than a verbal promise. The helper must have sufficient force.

On the other hand, turn to the eighteenth chapter of the Book of Judges and you will find another type of war-maker with whom you must deal. The children of Dan have started out on a freebooting expedition. Their reasoning is simple. "In those days there was no king in Israel, and in those days the tribe of the Danites sought them an inheritance to dwell in." So they sent out spies who "came to Laish and saw the people that were therein, how they dwelt in security after the manner of the Zidonians, quiet and secure; . . . and they were far from the Zidonians."

What happened? The Children of Dan "came unto Laish, unto a people quiet and secure, and smote them with the edge of the sword; and they burned the city with fire. And there was no deliverer, because it was far from Zidon."

One would like to say that that is only ancient history, and that such things do not happen now to any small nation that lies quiet and secure. Unhappily the facts do not bear out this pious wish.

The Children of Dan have their logic too. They reason, "Laish is weak, we are strong; therefore we will take it for ourselves. We need territory for expansion. We can get it by the strength of our own arms."

If such wars of aggression are to cease, the Danites must be confronted with a power which they have learned to respect. When they say arrogantly, "We will," the quick answer comes, "You cannot." Moreover, this restraining power must be wise enough to consider and redress the real grievances of the Danites. If they cannot take the means of livelihood by force, there must be some just means provided for them.

The question of keeping the peace resolves itself into a question of power. We must find a power that can satisfy the legitimate desires of men, and repress their illegitimate and abnormal desires. This is the purpose of social organization. It is based on the principle that all men are stronger than some men. If we could find what is good for all men, and then get all men to see these things which belong to the common good, we should have the power to enforce peace.

Such agreement as to what constitutes the common good is still far off, but mankind has been moving toward it. Wherever two or three are met together for a common purpose there is movement away from anarchy. People have learned to say, " We."

Two notable triumphs of peace principles have taken place — the family and the nation.

The family is a most interesting institution to study because in any community we may see it in all stages of development, from the pure despotism, in which the physically strongest rules, to the ideal coöperative commonwealth. But after ages of experiment it has been found that the highest forms have proved the stronger.

The same thing has proved true in regard to the national groups. The free republic has proved to be one of the strongest of political organizations. It is the triumph of reason over brutal passions. It involves the principle of arbitration as opposed to the trial by battle. Men of different creeds, callings, and education are enabled to live together in a certain territory without resort to violence. The weaker party is not crushed, but is safeguarded in its fundamental rights. Moreover, ways have been invented for radical changes in policy. Every four years the people of the United States may

have a political revolution of the first magnitude
— the party in power is driven out in a single
day and the insurgents are installed without the
firing of a shot.

Human nature is not transformed, but reason
determines the way in which social forces may
work. The marvelous thing is that these ar-
rangements are not upheld merely by the idealists who devised them. The free institutions are
supported by the irresistible might of all citizens. The hard-headed and narrow-minded partisans who ordinarily oppose each other bitterly
will on the instant unite in defense of the Constitution. Anarchy has only to be recognized
to be crushed.

It is from this vantage-ground won by past
effort that we can best use our power for the
suppression of international warfare as it now
exists. The peace-lover makes a strategical mistake when he appeals merely to the individual
conscience and treats war as personal prefer-
ence. Very few individuals prefer going to war
to other forms of human activity. It is as members of a nation and in obedience to the social
conscience that they sacrifice their lives.

It is to the social conscience and the patriotic impulse that we must appeal if international war shall give way to something better.

The time has come when people of all nations are asking how that which is most precious in their nationality can be preserved. They have tried to preserve these things by each nation arming in its own defense. At last the weight of necessary armament becomes intolerable. And when the long-prepared-for conflict comes, the victor and the vanquished fall in common ruin.

Certainly it is not beyond the wit of man to devise a way by which the power of all nations could be put behind a few simple laws which all recognize as just and for the common good. Our notions of national sovereignty must be revised, so that we shall recognize some limits. So we have had to define the liberty of the individual before we could have a nation strong enough to safeguard that liberty.

It has taken time and ceaseless effort to build up a government of the people. It will take more time and greater effort to bring order out of the present international anarchy. But the same forces which have worked hitherto must be used in the task that awaits us. We are still in a world where "ignorant armies clash by night." It is our task to dispel that ignorance. One thing we know and that is that when men are able to see their real interests they will see that they cannot be secured except by world-wide coöperation.

THE END